What Think Ye?

What Think Ye?

Essays for Twenty-First Century
Leaders, Pastors, and Church Musicians

Bob Burroughs

RESOURCE *Publications* • Eugene, Oregon

WHAT THINK YE?
Essays for Twenty-First Century Leaders, Pastors, and Church Musicians

Copyright © 2012 Bob Burroughs. All rights reserved. Except for brief quotations in critical publications or reviews, no part of this book may be reproduced in any manner without prior written permission from the publisher. Write: Permissions, Wipf and Stock Publishers, 199 W. 8th Ave., Suite 3, Eugene, OR 97401.

Resource Publications
An Imprint of Wipf and Stock Publishers
199 W. 8th Ave., Suite 3
Eugene, OR 97401
www.wipfandstock.com

ISBN 13: 978-1-62032-298-7
Manufactured in the U.S.A.

Contents

	Preface	xi
1	**First Corinthians 13—Love**	1
2	**Leadership**	
	The Lamp of Excellence	3
	Seven Hints to Become a Better Leader	5
	Vision and Passion	6
	Leadership Tips	6
	First Things First	7
	Leadership Do's and Don'ts	9
	Change Is the Great Inevitable	10
	Signs Your Leadership Style Is in Trouble	10
	A Good Leader	11
	The More People You Involve to Help, the Stronger Your Support Base Will Be!	12
	Stay the Course!	12
	Value Skills	13
	Questions to Ponder	14
	The Fine Art of Deception	14
	Helpmates	16
	Affirmation	16
	Everyone Has a Theory	17
	Uncommon Effort	17

The Journey Has Begun!	19
Innovation	20
Consecrate Yourselves, for Tomorrow	22
The Sky Is Not Falling	25
It Seems to Me	27
Should You or Should You Not?	28
The Role of a Teacher	30

3 Personal Attitude

Risk It!	33
Your Temper: Don't Lose It!	34
Thankfulness	35
Respect	36
Time	36
Find the Time	37
Ten Ways to Earn Respect	38
Attitude Determines Success	38
Climate Control	39
Climate Control Takes Intentionality	40
Sad versus Happy	41
Write It Down!	42
Want to Know a Secret?	43
Are You a Reader?	44
The Joy Factor	44
Habits	46
Where Do You Go to "Fill Up"?	47
Words	48
Character	49
Dignity	50
Choices	53

A Zeal He Does Not Own	54
Don't Make It—Fake It	55
Fellowship of the Saints	56
Music Shapes Us	58
Planning for Fall and Spring	59
Choose Your Ruts Carefully, and Don't Run out of Gas	61
Doing More Than Expected in Your Job Description	63

4 Email Etiquette

Email Etiquette	65
Avoiding Email Faux Pas	67
The Ten Commandments of Email	68

5 Success . . . Is Just Around the Corner!

Success	69
Three Rules for Success	70
Focus!	71
Successful versus Unsuccessful People	72
Top Five Secrets of Being Happy	73
If at First You Don't Succeed, Try a Different Way	74
Motivation: The Big "Mo"	75
Leisure Time	76

6 Stress . . . Will Take Its Toll

Stress	79
Stress Reducers	80
Ten Things to Learn from Criticism	82
Balance or Burnout	83
Keep Yourself Pure	84

| | Is Your Life at Flood Stage? | 85 |
| | Hurry Sickness | 87 |

7 Ten Leadership Mantras for Success

1. The two best-kept secrets of leadership — 89
2. The tendency of the masses is toward mediocrity. — 90
3. Have the courage to say "No." "No" is a complete sentence! — 92
4. The higher you are in the leadership chain, the less truth you will hear. — 93
5. When the horse is dead, dismount. — 94
6. The person in the organization who communicates clearest the vision is often perceived to be the leader. — 95
7. When you stop asking questions, you stop learning. — 96
8. Always play to your strengths. Delegate your weaknesses. — 98
9. Learn every thing you can from everyone you can whenever you can. — 98
10. Character is not made in crisis. It is only exhibited. — 100

8 Worship—Prayer—Church Concepts

The Mystery of Worship	103
The Art of Worship	104
Three Pitfalls of Worship	110
Worship Preferences	112
White to Black	113
The Purist	115
Economy-Driven Worship?	116
Hymns: Yesterday, Today—But Tomorrow?	118
Contemporary Music: Here to Stay or Soon Gone?	120
Thirteen Critical Issues for the Twenty-First Century	123
Creative Ways to Pray	124

Where Were These Words Spoken?	126
Princess Diana and Mother Teresa	127
This Isn't Your Father's Oldsmobile, or the Church as We Know It May Be in Trouble	127
Disney versus Church	130
A New Species of Worship Leader Has Emerged	132
Hymnody	133
Creativity	135

Preface

What Think Ye? Essays for Twenty-First Century Leaders, Pastors, and Church Musicians is, first and foremost, a leadership book, with to-the-point chapters that deal with the important leadership and musicianship issues for the twenty-first century. We are in new territory these days, and ministry isn't what it used to be. It's not your grandfather's style of leadership any more! We are treading in new territory that will require creative and innovative thinking. It will require ways to do ministry differently than what it used to be! This book will give you ideas as to how to do this.

The book also contains advice and lessons that can provide the reader new insights into ministry. It also contains food for thought and ministry leadership short-cuts that will be of value to church and school musicians, pastors, church staff and lay people who are involved and interested in leadership.

Distinguishing features of this book include short chapters that offer outside-the-books wisdom and suggestions on a variety of leadership subjects and styles. Not everyone leads in the same fashion. This book will help the reader zero in on helps, hints and comments that will boost the leadership appeal.

What Think Ye? is an easy read, but will take some digestion time to ponder and think about the subject matter in many of the chapters. It can be an excellent book for colleges, universities and seminaries that teach classes in church music ministry, as well as a gift book for leadership personnel in the ministry to which the reader has been called.

So, what think ye?

one

First Corinthians 13 Love

Paraphrased by Bob Burroughs

Though I shadow conduct with the very same strokes and imitate the style of the great conductors or use the actual baton of Robert Shaw, and have not love, I feel as if I am conducting in 3/4 time for a 4/4 song.

And though I have the gift of perfect pitch and understand all the mysteries of music theory, know every important date in music history and can even sing every voice part with absolute accuracy, can relate to the members of the youth choir, even with a fading hair line, and have not love, I am a beginner in the grand orchestration of life.

And though I think I teach my choirs what they need to know about relating to and loving God through the power of music, and though I try to teach them to read the right notes, and though I never copy any music without first obtaining written permission from the publisher, and even though I would never dream of copying a CD for my own use, and have not love, I find myself in violation of God's copyright on my life.

Love suffers long and is kind, even to those in my choir who never quite hit the right pitch.

Love does not envy my music minister neighbor or his program at First church. Love does not allow my spirit to become that of a musical elitista purist, a church music snob. Love is not a puffed-up imitation of the real thing.

Love does not stand alone. Love will not allow me to have a private church fortress mentality, seeking to minister to only those who are lovely, *clean, or active members. Love does not become easily provoked in rehearsals, is always willing to help those who miss important rehearsals, and is willing to stay after choir practice and minister to the flock.*

Love rejoices in the musical successes of others, applauds those who are growing in ministry, celebrates with those who are having golden opportunities thrust upon them, and weeps with those who have needs that cannot be shared with just everyone.

Love never goes flat or sharp, or even stays in unison, but breaks out into full harmony as life unfolds before me. Whether there be great and successful music ministries, they shall eventually fail. Whether there be regular rehearsals, full of anxious people, waiting to be taught, they will cease. Whether there be friendships, they will also vanish away.

For we know all the parts and we try to teach all the parts, accurately and with good taste. But when He who is the Perfect Musician comes, then we who struggle so hard to teach music skills will be done away with in favor of the Master Musician.

When I was a child, I sang as a child. I learned music skills as a child. I dreamed of my future before me as a child, dreaming of what God would have me to be in His kingdom. But when I became a grown-up, I realized that all these childish dreams were but foolish without the touch of the Master Musician.

Now, there abides faith: the song of a bird that senses the dawn and begins to sing in the darkness

There abides hope: springing eternal with every new psalm, hymn and spiritual song that sings of God's great glory and majesty.

There abides love: the magnificent force that drives us to the foot of the Cross.

The greatest of these?

Love.

two

Leadership

The Lamp of Excellence

IN THE LATE 1980S, over coffee one evening, one of the major heroes in my life said these words to me: "Bob, the 'golden age of church music' is almost over. The 'lamp of excellence' is about to go out."

That friend was the late James D. Woodward, and was he ever correct—a prophet in his own time. From this perspective, I know that he meant "the golden age of American church music, usually led by choirs of all ages," but I believe the sense of what he said is still the same. Many of you will remember Woodward and his influence in church music of the 1970s and 1980s. He was one of the finest conductors that ever lived, and he directed all his work, including major productions, from memory. He is missed to this day.

But true to his prediction, the "lamp of excellence" is still slowly dimming, and just like a fine mist, it will soon be too difficult to recapture once it is gone. I think that excellence is a state of mind. One does excellence because a burning desire is there to make it happen. One does excellence because of the call to music ministry and the desire to lead God's people to a higher plane.

Marva Dawn wrote these words: "We are to feed the sheep, not entertain the goats."

Recently, the famed composer, Samuel Adler, professor at the Juilliard School and professor emeritus at Eastman School of Music, spent a week at Samford University, Birmingham, Ala., as composer-in-residence.

What Think Ye?

During this week, he lectured daily as well as directed concerts of his music. In one session with the students, he said:

> "Some who attend music school apparently believe that love of music and talent can substitute for a rigorous education in music theory and history. This is the problem faced in most music schools. It is not enough to sing beautifully, play the right notes or love a piece of music. It is your duty to find out what makes this piece of music tick because you cannot sing it, you cannot play it unless you really know what's in it. A robot can play a Beethoven sonata, but no computer can do what you can do after you really know something about what you are doing."

He is right on target. When a student enters a music school, he becomes one of a large group of musicians who are as good or better than he is and he must prove himself worthy to be there. This means, first and foremost, a thorough and solid background in music theory! It is the baseline for all other music disciplines. These days, it seems conductors/directors seem to ignore things in the music that are so obvious. Such simple things as a missed note in a melodic pattern or an incorrect and passed over rhythm may signal to choir members that the director is either not aware the note was missed or doesn't wish to take the time to fix it. Your lamp is beginning to dim! Singing an anthem or playing an instrumental piece when it is not ready is a sure sign of a diminishing lamp. Below are some very basic suggestions that might inspire you to consider how bright your lamp may be:

- Never allow the choir/orchestra/ensemble to just get by. Demand excellence from your singers and players. Quality belongs to the Lord! No matter what the type of music or worship style in which you are involved, the music should be done as well as the choir/orchestra/ensemble is capable of producing, and you should not settle for anything less, even if you have to postpone a piece for a week or two. Your people will come to respect you for this stance.

- Set yourself a timeline on certain pieces, beginning up to six months or a year in advance. Keep checking it and working it so you are aware weekly where the piece is in process. The first fall rehearsal is when plans must be made to make it a huge success. A timeline will help with these details. Sometimes, church musicians are not the best detail people, and things can fall through the cracks.

The answer for this one is simple: Get help!

- Trust your administrative assistant to keep you on track.
- Trust your spouse with details, but of course, you have to share your dreams and concepts with him or her.
- Trust your choir officers, your staff and your personal mentors.
- If all else fails, trust yourself.

Find a personal mentor, a person you can trust to help you with your lamp of excellence, someone who will be honest and from whom you can take constructive criticism. Ask for these times comments often. Do not to take offense, but see how the comments might improve and strengthen your work, ministry and musicianship, and keep the flame aglow and bright in your lamp of excellence.

God is in the details. This Holy God, our Redeemer, Creator of the universe, and our Abba/Father deserves excellence in everything we do, say and conduct.

What think ye?

Seven Hints to Become a Better Leader

1. Use obstacles to your advantage. Never give in or give up easily.
2. Stay true to your vision. Without a vision, there is no leadership.
3. Create your own opportunities. No one else will create them for you.
4. Think big . . . bigger than those you lead.
5. Find your own solutions. Good solutions take thought, energy, and fortitude.
6. Treat those who whom you lead as a resource. People will be willing to help and assist if they feel appreciated and feel as if they are accomplishing something in the process.
7. Challenge the status quo! Never accept what is! Always look for what can be!

What think ye?

Vision and Passion

One of the key watchwords of today's church leadership should be vision. Vision is the ability to see what is not yet here. If our vision comes from God, then we must also have a passion for it. Passion fuels vision! If you don't have an emotional fire and heartfelt enthusiasm known as passion, you probably won't have true vision.

There are also passion destroyers that can keep you from having the passion that God desires us to stir in the hearts of our people—and even within our own hearts. These passion destroyers include:

- Bitterness: a bitter heart and spirit quenches the Spirit
- Disobedience to the will of God for your lives
- Distraction: anything getting in the way of your passion and vision
- Ego trips: one of the great stumbling blocks to a great ministry
- Lack of focus. If you can't focus, how do you expect your people to focus?
- Physical fatigue from overworking, overeating, overstressing, and not overcoming
- Selfish greed: everything that is done is done, cleverly disguised for "me" and not for the Kingdom
- Unwillingness to make painful changes, afraid to take a new step or offer a new challenge for fear of rejection.

What think ye?

Leadership Tips

> Lord, when I am wrong, make me willing to change.
> When I am right, make me easy to live with.
> So strengthen me that the power of my example will far exceed
> the authority of my rank.

A positive attitude may not directly change your circumstances, but it will change the way you respond to the circumstances. The responses of leadership people who are positive are likely to be:

- Active. Not always waiting, but doing.
- Solution-oriented. Always looking for answers.
- Generous toward others. Always giving and rarely seeking for themselves.
- Involving others in a task. Doesn't try to do everything themselves.
- Immediate/timely response to problems. Doesn't let issues pile up.
- Rooted in dignity and respect. Gives the person the benefit of the doubt.

Positive leaders are much more likely than negative leaders to turn their ideas into positive behavior. Positive behavior, in turn, does change circumstances, and nearly always, for the better. In order to grab hold of a slippery problem and rise above it, first, grab hold of a positive thought.

Leadership people work hard on their disposition!

What think ye?

First Things First

Leaders prioritize their time, perhaps not even realizing that in their choice of time, they are doing exactly what they want to do because it is tied to their personal purpose.

What leaders think is important is where they are going to spend the majority of their time!

Every person on the earth has the same amount of time per day and per week. Regardless of wealth or station in life, no one has less or more time.

Leaders are stressed at every level by people continually asking for their time, and most leaders have a very difficult time in saying the magic word: "No." Leaders fear that if they say "No," they won't be asked again, or they might hurt someone's feelings, or the opportunity just seems to be too good to turn down, or they think one more thing in an already crowded schedule won't hurt, or they think someone else won't do it as well as they can do it. Leaders learn to say "No." It gets easier with practice.

Leaders should be prepared to notice negative and subtle changes in family or job, which are brought on by too much outside responsibility. Some of these changes might include:

What Think Ye?

- Irritability
- Anger
- Ignoring people
- Sharp words
- Loneliness
- Frustration
- Fear
- Added stress

A leader should to list the important things in his life and adhere to that list religiously! High priorities for good leaders should be:

1. Quality time In personal devotions. It's hard to lead without instructions from the Boss.
2. Quality time with renewal and updating with the leader's best disciplines. A leader can't give and give without some renewal and inspiration from an outside source.
3. Quality time with spouse, away from children: long walks, reflective, romantic times often.
4. Quality time with children; ice cream after school, special Saturday breakfast, ball games.
5. Quality time with grandchildren: sending letters and cards, making phone calls, getting them surprises.
6. Quality time spent on the position or job: making sure your best shot is involved in your job and you aren't giving the best away somewhere else.
7. Recreation: an absolute must for leader survival.

Things a leader might consider pruning:

1. Assignments that are low items on the personal scale
2. Activities taking the leader away regularly from family and job
3. Activities that are similar in nature and can be cut without concern
4. Time spent on things not important to family, job, or calling

Just because the boss is a "work-a-holic" is no reason others have to follow in those footsteps and be on the course for an early heart attack, family problems, nervous break-down, job stress, and more! Time is a priority. Use it wisely!

What think ye?

Leadership Do's and Don'ts

Do help other people see the benefit of the project.

Don't talk about yourself any more than necessary. Praise others—not yourself!

Do discuss performance and never personality.

Don't be negative. Being around negative persons can drain your batteries.

Do be positive, but not dogmatic; candid, but not blunt.

Don't be overly diplomatic or sugary.

Do aim at consistency. Do not to play favorites.

Don't try to manipulate people. Manipulators are phonies, and phonies usually finish last.

Do know the strongest motivations of your people so you can effectively lead.

Don't say anything to someone you can't say with sincerity.

Do practice human kindness as well as tough mindedness.

Don't be sarcastic. Sarcasm stems from weakness.

Do let your enthusiasm show.

Don't forget the other person's point of view.

Do recognize the power of suggestions, and listen carefully.

Don't confuse activity with results.

Do keep abreast of training opportunities to make yourself a better leader.

Don't ever stop learning!

What think ye?

What Think Ye?

Change Is the Great Inevitable

Leaders can no longer pretend change is not going to happen around them and their organizations, just as some, in the early days of space travel, refused to believe that people had actually been to the moon, and believed it was all a fake. Church ministry leader must accept, and even embrace change, if they are to impact their people and community.

In his book, *Trigger Points,* Michael Kami described future-oriented leaders as detectives, architects and agents of change

As with Columbus, uncharted waters should be a challenge instead of a dreaded fear. Future-active leaders will stay abreast of the changes in their world. They will try to perceive things the way they really are and then figure out how best the church can respond. Of course, the Message is unchanging, but the methods must change.

Remember Richard Blanchard's words: "Doing today's work—with yesterday's tools—will put you out of business—tomorrow."

What think ye?

Signs Your Leadership Style Is in Trouble

- First comes the sniffles, then comes the cold.
- First comes the thunder and lightening, then comes the storm.
- First comes the road noise, then comes the flat tire.

Warning signs are wonderful things because they do just that: warn of approaching trouble!

There are warning signs, too, in leadership that may not have come to fruition as yet. Here are just a few:

- People have slowed down in following your leadership. An old cowboy saying: "When you are riding out in front of the herd, look back ever so often to see if they are still following you." This is especially true in leadership. You can get so far ahead (or behind) your "followship" that they give up! You may be doing too much and they can't keep up and become discouraged. You may be doing too little and they are not challenged and say, "Why bother?" Ever so often, in a group meeting, rehearsal or committee meeting, place a 3 x 5 card in every chair with a pencil. Let your people become acquainted with the idea that when they see this card, they have the freedom to write you a personal note with no holds barred. In the process, you will learn a lot! Trust your people. They aren't usually wrong.

- People seem to be complaining all the time. What are they complaining about? Listen carefully to them. Are there too many new things going on? Are there too many old things on the agenda? Are your meetings boring? Do the meetings never change or present anything new? Are you too aloof from the members and don't spend time with them? Do you pop in just in time for the meeting and then pop out and are gone? Listen to your people.

Learn to read the signs!

What think ye?

A Good Leader

All who are in leadership ministry have their plates more than full. Agree?
Therefore, in order to be successful, fulfilled and true to our calling, we must have:

- A heart for the leadership ministry, or do not accept the position
- A willingness to ask for help and assistance. There are people out there just waiting to be asked to assist.
- The ability to know how to shout and how to cry; often, do both.
- A passionate commitment to the cause, or you will not draw much commitment from others.
- The strength to walk up the hill, sometimes alone.
- A plan. He who does not have a plan has little chance of succeeding.
- A willingness to seek training to improve basic skills.
- A sense of God's leadership in your own personal life.

What think ye?

What Think Ye?

The More People You Involve to Help, The Stronger Your Support Base Will Be

I know and you know people who are trying to do it all—everything, the whole enchilada—by themselves, and their ministry is severely hampered because only one person is involved, and only one person is doing all the work!

- People want and desire to help and assist.
- People want to be asked to be a part of something that is worth their time and effort.
- People want to serve and be productive.
- People want to be made to feel important and to believe that what they are doing is worthwhile.

The load is easier to carry if three or fifteen people are helping do the task. There are people in your area of responsibility who are just waiting to be asked to serve, and they will astound you with what they are capable of doing when their skills are unleashed and turned loose to do it.

You can't do it all! Nor, should you! Let the people serve with you.

What think ye?

Stay the Course!

Highly successful people know where they are going, how they will get there, and why they are going there. They are not easily distracted, even by opportunities to change direction or focus. Success in a program or ministry does not come from chasing every opportunity, now matter how real it seems. It certainly does not result from seeking a quick fix to the situation.

Successful people quickly adopt new tools, but they rarely change their direction. While they may immediately understand the advantages of new technology or try a new technique, they endure, persevere, and wisely stay the course!

As a leader, your time is quickly eaten up with details, and many times, you are left with hardly anything to give to the family, including time, energy, creativity, and even leadership. It becomes imperative that you see ways to refresh your skills as often as you can, so you can stay "in the loop," fresh, alive, and alert.

- Do not ever think you know it all.
- Do not be too busy in your ministry to miss a training opportunity.
- Remember: you are one of God's chosen ones in the highest activity we know—leadership of God's people!

What think ye?

Value Skills

In a recent *USA Today* survey, people were asked to give their opinion of the top "value skill" of leadership. Here are the results:

1. Honesty. This seems to always be a concern for leadership. Good leaders are honest!
2. Integrity. Leaders have moral and spiritual integrity.
3. Commitment. How can a leader expect other to be committed if the leader is not totally on board?
4. Loyalty. Will the leader "go to the wall" for the project or presentation?
5. Fairness. How truly fair are our leaders in all venues of responsibilities?
6. Concern for others. Is there a real interest and concern for followers?
7. Respect. Does the leader have genuine respect for followers? If not, why not?
8. Obedience to the law. Does the leader "bend all the rules" to suit self?
9. Pursuit of excellence. Is excellence a part of the fiber of the being of the leader?
10. Personal accountability. Without this, a leader is leading no one ... but self.

What think ye?

What Think Ye?

Questions to Ponder

When I am involved in a conference, I often ask someone this question: "What do you wish to be doing 10 years from now?" and the look on the person's face is obvious. It says, "I've never thought about that!"

Now might be a good time to consider the following questions:

- Where do you want to be and what do you want to be doing 10 years from now? Think hard about it! You'll be 10 years older. Your family will be 10 years older. Your car will be 10 years older. You will have been in your job (f you still have it) for 10 years.

- What are the plans you are making for the future—for the "nest egg" in retirement—for what you had always dreamed God would have you do? Don't wait until you are older to begin an annuity program! Do it now!

- Where are you on the call from God upon your life? Is it still fresh and alive in your life and in your ministry?

- What are the renewal plans you are making in this new year that will make you a better leader, worship leader, conductor, spouse or parent?

- From where do you expect to get some renewed energy and inspiration for your ministry?

- What is your number one priority right now? Think carefully before you answer. Did your answer surprise you? Do you need to rethink priorities?

What think ye?

The Fine Art of Deception

Deception enters our lives in a wide variety of sources. It comes into our lives, ministries, families, staff and situations as subtle as the frog in the kettle, and before we know it, we have been fooled and deceived! Deception is a tool of the Evil One, the greatest deceiver of all time.

The fine art of deception convinces us:

- We know as much as we need to know and, therefore, it is not necessary to refresh, retool, rethink or renew.
- We are about as good in our skill level as is required by our job or the church and, therefore, it would be a waste of time to do any further study or refinement of our skills.
- The only important things that happen in the Kingdom of God happen within the walls of my church fortress and nothing of real value happens outside these church walls.
- We do not have meaningful fellowship with other leaders or people simply because we just don't have the time. There's just too much happening in our own fortress.
- We can't be bothered being a faculty member of a summer youth or children's camp because the church would not survive without us being around for even five days. That is also why we never take a day off or a real vacation.
- No one will ever know if I visit a computer website that might be a bit shady. After all, no one will ever know and, I'm not hurting anyone.

You see, the fine art of deception is really subtle; it is true art form. Before we know it, we find ourselves caught deeper in this web than we ever intended. Our leadership skills become stale. Our staff senses our leadership skills are lacking a fresh inspiration. Our leadership skills lack authority and conviction. Our spiritual walk seems to be dormant, and we find ourselves not being able to hear the still small voice of God.

In a word, we find ourselves becoming mediocre, which is average or moderate, and we began to sense something is wrong with this picture.

Defense is the best weapon against the fine art of deception.

We must use defense: alertness, listening, communication, renewal and spiritual strength, and extremely important, we must spend quality and consistent time with our spouse. This can be the salvation factor.

As Barney Fife used to say: "Deception? Nip it! Nip it in the bud."

What think ye?

Helpmates

A spouse plays a very important role in the life of any person involved in leadership of any kind; without spouse support and influence, a vital part of the leadership ministry is always absent.

This doesn't mean that spouses have to necessarily be totally involved—doing everything, working in several positions in the church, and trying to keep house, grow healthy kids and be the one who always gets the groceries and takes out the garbage!

It just means that spouses need personal attention—outside the church realm of life! Praying together as a couple is a grand place to begin. Dating once a week, every two weeks or at least once a month, is a grand idea, with no business talk allowed! Sharing your ideas and dreams with the spouse is a very good way to try them out and see if they will fly.

Make sure your spouse is involved with you in your leadership ministry as a support person. Make sure your spouse knows what is going on in your life and feels a valuable part of the ministry, or there will be problems, perhaps major problems, down the road.

What think ye?

Affirmation

Affirmation to our spouse and children will help them have maturity and self-confidence.

The same is true of your leadership staff! If you love on them, compliment often, affirm what they are doing that is right and good, and encourage them as they accomplish something special, they will be more inclined to trust you and be more faithful to the task.

If you are always harping on them, fussing, and raking them over the coals, they will soon tire of that kind of behavior and look elsewhere for a place to serve. Many, I fear, receive that kind of treatment at their secular job and don't need to come to church and get it there also.

A positive word goes a long way! I know someone who begins staff meetings each week by affirming staff members, telling them what they are doing right and affirming their good points. His respect continues to grow.

It will also work for you.

What think ye?

Everyone Has a Theory

Have you ever thought about it? Almost everyone has a theory about something, an answer or a solution to all the problems of the world. If "they" would only do this or if "they" would only do that, everything in the world would be OK.

To be perfectly honest, I'm always a bit leery of those kinds of people! To me, they are sort of like the "ultra-religious" people, wearing their religion on their shirtsleeves or faces and always conversing in "God-talk." Even in the midst of both good and not-so-good times, these people seem to have all the answers, given directly from God—or so they make me feel!

In truth, we are all seekers. We are all on the journey. We are all in transit. Not one of us has all the answers! Sometimes I wonder if I have an answer for anything—period. Jesus encouraged His followers to be gentle, loving, load-bearing for brothers and sisters, willing servants, caring for the less fortunate and, of course, true to ourselves as well as to Him.

Everyone has a theory.

My theory is this:

> *Do not let this Book of the Law depart from your mouth; meditate on it day and night, so that you may be careful to do everything written in it. Then . . . you will be prosperous and successful. Have I not commanded you? Be strong and courageous. Do not be terrified; do not be discouraged, for the Lord your God will be with you wherever you go.* (Joshua 1:9)

What think ye?

Uncommon Effort

> "The truth is most people have a better chance to be 'uncommon' by effort—than by natural gifts. Anyone could give that effort in his or her chosen endeavor, but the typical person doesn't, choosing to do only enough to get by." (Tony Dungy, *Quiet Strength*, Tyndale Books, p. 29)

This quote is by the former Indianapolis Colts Football Coach, Tony Dungy, and it literally jumped out at me! I have seen this happen many times in my 56+ years of ministry in the local church, in the university setting and among leadership! Both young people and adults, who have been given so much natural ability to do what God has called them to do or to be, have chosen instead to walk the wide highway of doing just enough to get by.

Read Dungy's statement once more, and then, let his words sink deep into your soul. Try to recall the times when you have chosen the wide road rather than pay the price to walk the narrow path of personal discipline.

These instances might help in your recall process:

- The student who fluffs off all semester, then hits the practice room the night before juries and memorizes three to four pieces out of the required 10 and hopes the faculty will call one of the ones memorized, instead of doing consistent work throughout the semester and being prepared to face the music.

- The musician who allows the choir or orchestra to get by singing or playing wrong notes, incorrect phrasing or ignores the composer's dynamic listings and instructions, allowing the choir or orchestra to sing or play at a constant forte level, with no thought whatsoever given to good musicianship, precision and preparing a piece to be offered to the glory of God.

- The young person, who has so many gifts and skills, feels led by a call from God, and works just hard enough to earn a final grade of C, when he knows C is average. We have far too many average people in ministry today as it is!

One cannot help but wonder if the one who has the gifts and skills to excel, but chooses instead to walk the wide highway of average, will someday turn to the narrow path of personal discipline and focus his gifts/skills where God had intended him to focus and become one of those extraordinary people who learns to excel in order to honor the Father, who demands only the best gifts, the best fruits, the top of the ladder.

What think ye?

The Journey Has Begun!

The time has come. We have embarked on a journey, a journey that will last 365 days, or 8,765 hours, 525,948 minutes and 31,556,926 seconds! Wow!

This journey is each New Year of our Lord. Ahead for each one of us lies:

- Possibilities to explore
- Dreams to be fulfilled
- Opportunities to grow in our calling by the God who chose us
- Family to love, nourish and cherish
- Music to find, rehearse, grow to love and perform
- Friendships to honor and respect

But, alas! Also, ahead of us there may be:

- Pain and suffering
- Loss of a loved one
- Serious injury or even death
- Financial struggles
- Personal battles
- Job insecurity
- Problems to solve that may be larger than life

In every New Year, which of these categories would you prefer?

Silly question, isn't it!? We would all prefer category number one, but we know that some of category number two will face us in a New Year.

The most interesting thing about the above time figures is that we all have the same amount of time with no exceptions. The number one excuse to be used in this coming year will be: "I just don't have the time." Poor excuse! Poor reasoning! Poor planning!

What do you plan to do with your days, hours, minutes and seconds in the New Year? How do you plan to enlarge your tent and stretch your stakes?

What Think Ye?

What? You have made no plans? You haven't given it much thought? You don't even know what you'll be singing this coming Sunday? You have made no plans for personal improvement and study? There are no plans to better yourself or your ministry? You don't usually plan ahead, but just let the year unfold as God would have it unfold?

Surely you jest! Surely this can't be true! You have 365 days to challenge yourself to be better, to fulfill God's gifts in the Kingdom, to stretch and grow, to love, to teach, to minister, and to laugh and weep with friends, church members and family.

The best may yet to come, regardless of how we look at it. A New Year offers change, challenge, creativity and cooperation. But if you allow it, it can also offer confusion, conflict and control that will not be part of God's plan for your life.

Go ahead! Make exciting plans for this New Year. It is not too late. Think about the weeks and months to come and how you can use them to become better at what you do; to become a better, more qualified minister; to become a better parent; to think creatively as to how you can challenge your people to be better worshipers and followers.

All this is within our grasp as we embark on the journey of a New Year!

What think ye?

Innovation

Innovation frees the dreamers, the creative ones and those who want to change things for the better, not so much for the sake of change, but for the sake of the Kingdom. The church has for too long been behind the times. The church has for too long been yesterday's news instead of the secondary headlines in the papers. It is high time that today's church steps up and become leaders in the communities and beyond. This can be done most easily through the magic of innovation coupled with sincere and meaningful prayers.

The following article attracted my attention and interest. I think it will do the same for you.

Granger Community Church, Granger, Ind., where Mark Beeson serves as senior pastor, has recently been rated as one of the most innovative churches in the country. Innovation must be a very important issue in this church. Beeson says there are three truths about innovation that relates to today's church:

1. Innovation means improvements are made within the rules. First, he says, learn the rules. Then, innovate for improvement.
2. Institutions do not exist for innovation. People do. E.M. Bounds said, "People are God's method." God uses visionaries and dreamers to introduce things new and different. Look for people with passion and who will think creatively and courageously!
3. Innovation can bring success, but it always costs! Any new idea will pay a price, because, as Aldous Huxley said, "The tendency of the masses is towards mediocrity."

The majority of people in any church or organization do not want to step out of the boat and disrupt the norm. They are content with the status quo. They will always resist change.

There is an art to innovation. It is a skill that can be learned. Guy Lawasaki's book, *The Art of the Start*, offers these innovation tips:

1. Make meaning. The three ways to do this are create good things, end bad things or perpetuate existing good things.
2. Make mantra. Don't write a 30-word mission statement that no one can remember. Select three to six words that tell clearly what you do.
3. Roll the DICEE. Great innovation is Deep, Intelligent, Complete, Elegant and Emotive.
4. Never fear polarizing people. Some will love it and some will hate it, but that's OK. If you try to make everyone happy, you end up with mediocrity.
5. Fix it! Once you've launched your innovation, now evolve it by fixing the bugs and tweaking it.
6. Don't let naysayers grind you down. They will tell you it can't be done, shouldn't be done and of course, isn't necessary. Ignore these people and press on with your dream.

What think ye?

What Think Ye?

Consecrate Yourselves, for Tomorrow

Those are words of great inspiration and challenge for me. Many of you know me from my Samford University and Palm Beach Atlantic University teaching days, or from my time as director of the Church Music Department for the Florida Baptist Convention, or as a composer. You may also remember that I am one who has always wanted to be in the midst of "amazing things." Even now in retirement, I still want to be a part of amazing things, trying to stay abreast in any way that I can and trying to keep myself fresh and up-to-date.

Once in a while, I play keyboards in our church praise band on a need basis. Desperate might be the better term! When I recently told a friend what I was doing, he said: "Well, I guess you can teach an old dog new tricks!"

I tell people I don't play notes, I just play chords!

What do the words, "amazing things," mean to you?

To me, they mean:

- If we consecrate ourselves anew each day and are faithful to the Father in Bible study and prayer, in private and/or with our families, He has promised that He will accomplish amazing things in us and in our ministries.

- If we trust Him for tomorrow, He will ensure that amazing things will happen in our ministries beyond our belief or imagination.

- If we take some chances and try some amazing things that might seem impossible at first, perhaps, through the power of the Holy Spirit, careful planning and the cooperation of God's people, they might come to fruition and surprise a lot of people in the process.

As leaders, we are in the continual process of mentoring people, whether we realize it or not and whether we want to or not. We are constantly in the eyes of our people, and our ministry leadership becomes positions of visual leadership and as well as practical education!

Certainly, ministry is a vital part of all that we do, but in the grandest sense, we are also educators as well as leaders. We are the ones who should be modeling for our people professionalism and quality in the highest sense of the word, every time, all the time and with as much energy as we can muster.

Leadership

It behooves us to make sure that everything that is done in our music ministry is accomplished in a first-class manner, and we should model this always for our people.

I heard someone say these words to a friend who does a yearly church music leadership conference: "I know that when I come to this conference, it will have your fingerprints of excellence all over it and I try not to ever miss something you have planned."

What a high compliment! In today's world and society, and in our various ministries we can no longer afford to "copy-and-paste" old programs into a new programs or new wine into old wine skins by simply changing the names! Our people can see through this very quickly.

Ken Blanchard made this great statement: "When the horse is dead, dismount!" That is such a great statement!

There lots of programs from which the church needs to dismount! If we stopped here and asked each of you to name only two in your church, each one could name two and maybe more! Churches seem to have a hard time letting go of anything once it has begun.

We can no longer turn over our anthem barrel and sing the same pieces we sang last year. There is too much wonderful, new and exciting literature being published today to stick with the same old music rehearsal after rehearsal, year after year. Your people deserve better! Of course, there is a place for the sugar stick anthems—those loved by director, choir and people—but to sing the same pieces every year begins to run thin.

I know a minister of music in anther state who has sung Jane Marshall's fabulous anthem, "My Eternal King," on Easter Sunday, for 29 years! Can't he learn a new anthem for the Easter season? And, he still looks at his music as the choir sings, as if it is new to him!

The church can no longer lean on its past laurels, recalling and claiming all of the good and successful times once experienced and then expect people to come and be a part of the church programs or our music ministry out of loyalty to the program. As I'm sure you are experiencing, there is no loyalty to the program. These days, there isn't much loyalty to anything!

Read this carefully: People in today's society do things for their reasons and not yours.

This is a very difficult lesson to learn in ministry.

We can no longer plan worship the same way week after month after year and expect our people to grow musically, spiritually and in community. If your liturgy, or as many call it, the order of worship, has not changed in the past month, you may be experiencing those dinosaur steps referred to in William Easom's grand book, which should be on the desk of every minister of music, *Dancing with Dinosaurs,* published by Abingdon Press. Get a copy and prepare to be surprised at what he thinks is our future in church music.

We can no longer expect our people to come to anything the church offers—be it music, worship or education—that is not presented in a professional manner. Television, movies, touring Broadway plays and musicals have spoiled our people into thinking that even their church should be professional in some ways, and they have the right to expect the best the church can offer.

Again, the currency of this new century is time. People no longer ask, "How much will this cost?" They now ask, "How much time will that take?"

We can no longer waste the time of our people in today's fast-paced society. They just don't have time for less-than-the-best.

They have a right to expect worship to begin on time and end on time, unless the Holy Spirit is active and alive in the service.

They have a right to expect committee meetings to begin on time and end on time.

People no longer have the luxury of free time. Everyone is busy in some respect, and the church is notorious for wasting the time of their people.

If what we are doing in our programming and ministry is not of real value to the people for whom the program is targeted and attendance is low and decreasing, then we are wasting their time, and the sharp people will be slow to return a second or third time! This is especially true of committees. It they are not accomplishing anything or even meeting once a quarter, drop them! What purpose are they serving in the Kingdom?

So, being concentrated and being open to the Father's direction in our lives will only come in the quiet moments we spend in fellowship with Him.

Remember: God was not in the fire, the flood, or the wind, but in the still small and gentle breeze. He will not wrestle for your attention.

Listen again, to the words found in Joshua 3:5: "Concentrate yourselves, for tomorrow, the Lord will do amazing things among you."

Hear the words of John Parker III, with music by Mark Hayes, published by Hinshaw Music:

> To love our God, the reason we live.
> To love our God, the highest call.
> Nothing satisfies our soul,
> gives life meaning, makes us whole
> For this purpose we were make:
> To Love Our God!

This sums it up nicely.

What think ye?

The Sky Is Not Falling

Contrary to the fable that is sailing rampant around the world these days, the sky is not falling. Chicken Little was wrong then, and he is wrong today. The sky is not falling! Things will eventually turn around. They turned around in the more difficult times of the past, and they will turn around in our time—but not before the peoples of the world go through hard times, a rethinking of resources, and begin to think with clear heads and hearts instead of jumping to conclusions over every issue that faces us.

Difficult to do? You bet!

Will there be some pain, sorrow and many questions during the process? Absolutely!

Is this current crisis going to cause us to reconsider lots of things we have taken for granted? Yes!

But the sky is not falling, and the world will not come to an end until the Lord God, Almighty says, "It is time. Bring Gabriel to Me. its time to sound the final call."

So what do we do in the meantime??

I am not claiming in any way to be the answer man for today's economic troubles, I assure you, but I have some thoughts for our consideration:

- Pray more.
- Trust God more.

What Think Ye?

- Love Him more
- Conserve and save resources.
- Hunt for bargains
- Spend less.
- Tithe.
- Give more.
- Believe.
- Knock. It shall be opened.
- Play.
- Rest.
- Love your family more.
- Exercise.
- Relieve stress.
- Work in the yard.
- Don't give up.
- Stay true to your call.
- Ban discouragement.
- Embrace hope.
- Help others
- Search for truth.
- Show mercy.
- Fight for justice.
- Live humbly.
- Be a person of grace.

Here's a hard thought for today's economy as it relates to church and school musicians.

Perhaps it may be time for music publishers and music distributors to consider cutting prices for a year or two. One major religious music publishing company recently told me they did not turn a profit in 2008, the first time in the history of the company; yet, they raised prices in their catalog in Fall 2008.

Churches are really being hit hard during this economic stress. My church, which has never been behind in budget before, recently found itself $200,000 behind budget, and it was only April! Other churches are facing similar financial downfalls. Some churches are putting ministers of music on half salary! So when did worship become economy-driven?

Soon, church financial leaders are going to begin saying things like, "Use the music you have in the library." Or, "We don't have the money to pay up to $2.00 for an anthem." Or, they may suggest, "Hey! Make copies. No one will ever know!" Or, "Here's your music budget. Use it wisely, for there will be no more money coming your way."

I'm thinking that reducing prices on octavos, collections, musicals, instrumental scores, and handbell scores in the short-term might go a long way in the public relations arena.

The sky is not falling. It just feels that way. But this, too, shall pass!

What think ye?

It Seems to Me

It seems to me ... that churches located in downtown areas provide many opportunities for service and ministry to the surrounding community. Medical clinics, clothing banks, counseling, food banks, child care and more are common in inner-city churches. But little participation from the surrounding community is obvious in weekly worship services. We may use words like: "You are most welcome here!" But, perhaps the worship style, decor and pulpit leadership as well as those in attendance might give indications that "We are so happy to do things for you, but you really are not one of us." (Comments are a summary on this topic by C. Michael Hawn.)

It seems to me ... that mega churches have few if any members living within even a one-mile radius of the church, meaning members have to drive to the church sometimes from long distances. With the price of gas sky-rocketing higher every day, the mega churches may begin to see declining attendance as well as declining income on a regular basis as people have to choose churches that are within a few blocks of their homes in order to save gas.

It seems to me . . . that those members of far-and-away churches still need to be ministered to if they remain members of the church, which puts great pressure on the church staff and church members to think of creative and innovative ways to provide ministry to far-and-away members. If people can't afford to get to the church, then the church has to get to the people via the Internet, email, house church services, music and sermons on CD or DVD and mailed to these members and other ways to minister creatively to this growing group of people.

It seems to me . . . these scenarios present an interesting predicament to church staff leadership, doesn't it? These present challenges could change the future of today's church. My speaker/wife, Esther, says "We've turned 'Go ye' to 'Y'all come!'" Perhaps, it is time to rethink what we are doing in the church and think more about getting outside the church.

What think ye?

Should You or Should You Not?

Should you, as a music minister, sing with the choir when you conduct? I know how it started with me! I served as part-time choir director at a very small church in the Asheville, N.C., area when I was a second-year student at Mars Hill College in the mid-1950s. The choir was small, as you might suspect, and there was only one tenor. The bass section was anchored by to Mars Hill College friends who enjoyed the hospitality of this wonderful church, as well as the food they had over the weekends! There were a good and faithful number of sopranos and altos.

So, on a given Wednesday night or Sunday morning when the one tenor was not present, I felt I had to sing tenor, as well as conduct, give cues, listen for incorrect notes and check balance—which, of course is next to impossible. Singing with the choir became a staple for me for a number of years until I realized:

1. I wasn't helping the choir; I was only hindering them by singing along and not paying attention to the myriad of things for which a conductor is responsible.

Leadership

2. No one ever told me that singing with the choir limited my abilities as a conductor.
3. I figured that everyone else did it, didn't they?

Wrong! Wrong! Wrong!

Here is some food for thought on this subject:

It is physically impossible for a conductor to hear the choir if he/she sings along with them, no matter how good a voice he/she has! It just can't be done. The "sound box" is the head and it resonates with the sounds from the conductor's voice, blocking out other sounds! There is no way then, a conductor can really know how the choir sounds or what vocal parts are being missed if the conductor chooses to sing along with the choir on a regular basis.

Good blend? "Forgetaboutit!" Good balance of parts? "Forgetaboutit!" It just won't happen with a singing conductor.

Some conductors have the notion that if they sing very loud, then that will encourage the choir (and congregation) to sing with more volume and power. This is especially not-so-good thinking if the conductor has a microphone! I've visited a few rehearsals where the choir room sound system is at peak because the conductor is singing along at full vocal volume, oblivious to notes being obviously missed but obviously enjoying hearing himself sing!

This is an interesting side fact: I've noticed that sometimes the singers (and congregation) quit singing because they can't hear anything but the leader. I was recently in a session where the leader was singing so loud with his "golden microphone" that I gave up singing and began observing other singers. Many had quit singing because there was no reason to continue. Whatever sounds they were making were lost in the "glory" of the leader's voice.

I seriously doubt that the conductor is aware that many choir members and the congregation are just not singing because of the volume from the leader's microphone. It is as if he/she is enjoying the glory and majesty of his voice (with closed or uplifted eyes), oblivious to those he/she is leading!

To be perfectly honest, if there were a choice, the choir members would choose for the conductor not to sing but rather to spend his/her time helping them to become better musicians, singers and blenders. If

What Think Ye?

you don't think this is true, ask the choir! Send around a questionnaire with this question: "Am I helping you when I sing with the choir?" You will be amazed at the response!

A conductor should not sing with his/her choir. A conductor should listen carefully and work out problems that are missed while trying to conduct and sing a solo concert at the same time.

What think ye?

The Role of a Teacher

It seems as if my life's journey has been in ten-year segments!

- In the 1960s, I was involved in the local church as a minister of music in three churches.
- In the 1970s, I taught freshmen music theory and was composer-in-residence at Samford University, Birmingham, Ala..
- In the 1980s, I freelanced, while serving two churches part time.
- In the 1990s, my journey led me back into teaching at Palm Beach Atlantic University, West Palm Beach, Fla., for five years.
- Then my life took a turn that I never anticipated or dreamed. I became the director of the Church Music Department, Florida Baptist Convention, Jacksonville, Fla., in 1994 and served eight years.

In each of these segments, I considered myself a teacher, a professor who desired to teach better and do more than was expected of me. My desire was to inspire, to communicate life beyond mediocre. In my college teaching, I tried to teach that earning a "C" in my class or any other class was average, and if one was really serious about his education, he or she needed to excel beyond average! There were and still are too many average people out there!

This verse from James 3:1 has been in my heart and mind for several weeks. I decided to share it with you. I think it speaks to all who are in any level of teaching, and in many ways, all who are in ministry are teachers of religion from a most high calling of God!

> *Don't be in any rush to become a teacher, my friends. Teaching is highly responsible work. Teachers are held to the strictest standards.*

Leadership

And none of us is perfectly qualified. We get it wrong nearly every time we open our mouths. If you could find someone whose speech was perfectly true, you'd have a perfect person, in perfect control of life. James 3:1–2

Many times, teachers/professors seem eager to tell students and others about their faults, shortcomings and failures, while seeming to forget or ignore the fact that we also have faults, shortcomings and failures. Teachers have the upper hand, don't you see? Students of all ages and in all kinds of learning situations know the teachers have a desire to be perfect, when we all know none of us are perfect. And in many cases, teachers hold grades as a weapon.

I remember once when I had my first class in second year music theory at Palm Beach Atlantic University, I was the "new kid on the block" and walked into a class room of 15 students who did not know me from Adam's housecat, had loved their former teacher who had died a month before of a heart attack while conducting the Thanksgiving performance of "Messiah," and who weren't willing to give me any slack!

About half way through the class, one of the students asked me a very difficult question, the kind that comes in second year theory! Caught off guard and realizing this was my first time to teach second year music theory, I could make up something that would have sounded really good, but true? I didn't know for sure! Instead, I chose to say this: "I'm sorry, Mitch. I don't know the answer to that question. I'll have it by the next class period," and went on teaching. The next class period, I had the answer, you can be assured!

Later that year, Mitch came to me and confessed, "Mr. B., I asked you that difficult question in theory class that day on purpose, Sir. I knew the answer, as did all the class, but I wanted to know if you were real and genuine and would give us a straight answer. You did just that! I have come to love and appreciate you for being honest with us!"

Scripture states that we who are teachers of religion, who should know better, do wrong, our punishment will be greater than it would be for others. We are all teachers of religion, if we have been called by God into our present field of ministry, and our punishment for doing wrong, without genuine repentance, will be greater than it would be for others.

What think ye?

three

Personal Attitude

Risk It!

To laugh is to risk appearing the fool.

To weep is to risk appearing sentimental.

To reach out to another is to risk involvement.

To express feeling is to risk exposing your true self.

To place your ideas and dreams before the crowd is to risk their loss.

To love is to risk not being loved in return.

To live is to risk dying.

To hope is to risk despair.

To try is to risk failure.

But risks must be taken.

The greatest hazard in life is to risk nothing.

The person who risks nothing does nothing, has nothing, is nothing.

He may avoid suffering and sorrow, but he simply cannot learn, grow, feel, love or live.

Only the person who risks is truly free.

What think ye?

What Think Ye?

Your Temper: Don't Lose It!

When a person loses his temper, one of the most common expressions used to describe the situation is "flying off the handle." This phrase refers to the head of a hammer coming loose from the handle as the carpenter attempts to use it. When this happens, several things occur as a result:

First, the hammer becomes useless. It is no longer good for the work for which it was designed. In like manner, when a person loses his temper, he also loses his effectiveness. Anything said may not be taken seriously and is likely to be unproductive.

Second, the hammerhead—twirling out of control—is likely to cause some type of damage to anything in its path. The person who loses his temper, whether he knows it or not, causes damage perhaps physically to people or objects in his way, and nearly always, emotionally to those who feel they are victims of uncontrolled wrath.

Third, the repair of both the hammer and the resulting damage will take time. The person who loses his temper may recover quickly, but the one who is the victim of a hot temper rarely recovers quite so quickly.

Temper is what gets most of us into trouble. Pride is what keeps us there!

In an old monastery near Bebenhausen, Germany, there are two pairs of deer antlers hanging on the wall, and the horns are interlocked. They were found in that position years ago. Apparently, two bucks had been fighting for territorial or herd rights, and their horns became jammed together and the bucks could not separate themselves. They died in that locked position, unable to find a way of cooperating so that on bended knees, both might be able to eat or drink and eventually free one from the other.

These locked horns are not unlike many relationships that can be found today in our homes, schools, jobs, and even churches. People become entrenched in certain positions over certain issues and angrily confront those who oppose them. In the process, they "lock horns" and seem unable to ask each other for forgiveness or find a mutual way of serving one another in love. Both parties in such a relationship suffer, and ultimately lose.

God, in His divine wisdom, granted each two ears for listening and one mouth for speaking. This seems to say that we should listen twice as much as we talk, and if we are listening more and talking less, the stress of "locked horns" will become less likely in our daily walk before the Lord.

Keep your temper today! Nobody else wants it. Proverbs 25:28 says: "He that hath no rule over his own spirit is like a city that is broken down, and without walls."

What think ye?

Thankfulness

There is always a season for thankfulness for all God has provided for His people, including:

- Those who believe and those who doubt,
- Those who are graced and those who feel ungraced,
- Those who have it all and those who have nothing,
- Those who want it all and those who want only a warm bed and a meal to survive.

God is ever with us—whether we be in pain and sorrow, joy and gladness, or peace and turmoil.

He is in the trenches with those who are fighting the battles of life. He is in the office complexes with those who are trying to stay ahead and those burdened down with overwork. He is in the homes where love and peace reign supreme, and He is in the homes where discord and lovelessness are rampant.

We can all be thankful for something—most of us for everything—and a few of us for just being alive another day.

Sometime during this day, pause to give an expression of gratitude to the Father for all the bounty that is yours, whether it be little or much.

What think ye?

What Think Ye?

Respect

A wonderful proverb attributed to the German people says: "We are too soon old . . . and too late smart."

What a great thought! In my early days of ministry, I often wondered how long it would take for me to gain respect. I wondered when deacons, pastors, staff, choir members and church leaders would begin to recognize that I did have something to say and to think I needed to say it.

Perhaps that was the problem! Maybe they were not ready to hear what I had to say at that time in my ministry, and maybe I wasn't really ready to have a platform to say anything—period!

I began to think of all the people whom I had a great amount of respect and why I respected them. I discovered that most of those dear people were older, more mature, sages, wise, perhaps beyond their years.

One such was my dear late friend, James D. Woodward. He taught me so much about the power of music, the thrill of conducting, and how to motivate a choir. He loved me in those early years when I was discovering who I was and what I had to contribute to the world of church music. He listened and gave me grand advice!

I discovered that the older one becomes, the more people tend to listen, ask for advice, and desire counsel. With maturity comes wisdom. With experience comes know-how. With longevity in ministry comes a stability that leads to security. Patience is a great teacher.

What think ye?

Time

The new poverty of the twenty-first century is time starvation! With this in mind, how are you handling the time God has given you—24-hours in a day? A good checklist of the time you spend each week would be to keep a time sheet like you used to do in college, and begin on Monday, putting down everything you do in the week and the time allotted. When you finish, you will be amazed at what you discover.

- How much quality time did you spend with your spouse?
- How much quality time did you spend with your children?

Personal Attitude

- How much actual time did you use planning and preparing the worship service for God's people?
- How much time did you spend in preparation for your main rehearsals?
- How much time did you spend taking care of your health?
- How much time did you spend dreaming and creating?
- How much time did you spend in spiritual and musical preparation for each rehearsal?
- How much time did you spend in prayer?
- How much time did you spend affirming, loving, and supporting your church and choir people?

My! Where did the time go?

What think ye?

Find the Time

As you prioritize your time each week, make sure you find the time

    ... to plan

    ... to dream

    ... to think

    ... to promote

    ... to minister

    ... to share yourself with someone else

    ... to prepare your music well

    ... to become a better conductor

    ... to become a better musician/minister

    ... to be an outstanding worship leader

    ... to work to improve the capabilities of your accompanist

    ... to get assistance and help where needed

    ... to read your Bible and pray

What Think Ye?

> ... to love children
>
> ... to kiss your wife
>
> ... to study to show yourself approved unto God.

What think ye?

Ten Ways to Earn Respect

1. Respect yourself. Know your strengths and weaknesses.
2. Give credit where it is due. Be lavish in giving away credit to others.
3. Don't be too familiar with your people. We all want to be loved and appreciated. Just be careful and very wise.
4. Criticize in private; commend in public.
5. Observe all the rules you expect everyone else to observe.
6. Don't make promises you can't fulfill.
7. Respect confidences. Keep it to yourself.
8. Be consistent. Don't be moody, and don't always give your personal burdens to others. They have enough burdens of their own.
9. Keep calm under the most trying of circumstances. We all want to run and hide at certain times, but we can't. Show confidence and people will catch it and want it.
10. Show enthusiasm and joy in your job. Delight in your position. Enjoy your people. Make the most and the best of every situation.

What think ye?

Attitude Determines Success

Your attitude will determine the success or failure of your day—believe it or not!

If you go about your job in a happy mood, jovial, smiling, eager and determined, your day will go better.

If you come into your job carrying extra baggage like personal or family problems, staff strife, and are up-tight and stressed, it will have a major impact on your day and upon those who are around you.

Therefore, it is absolutely imperative that you rid yourself of all stress as much as possible so that you can inspire, challenge, and encourage your people to be better at what they do for the Kingdom.

Side remarks, personal jokes, and inappropriate humor are all out of place in a workplace.

Keep your personal feelings to yourself and strive to challenge your people to be better than they are, and they will—under your direction if you prepare your day free of personal stress.

Never carry personal baggage into your day! Enjoy your people! Love them. Challenge them. Encourage them. Stretch them to be better than they think they can be.

You can do it—with the right attitude!

What think ye?

Climate Control

Have you ever noticed that every home has its own unique fragrance or climate sometimes called ambiance? Perhaps, you can recall the particular aroma of the home in which you grew up or the smell in the home of your grandparents, such as fresh baked bread!

Application of this analogy can also be made to the church where you serve as a leader. There is a climate, yes, even a fragrance and an ambiance, that your team members get when they are with you and under your leadership. They may not be able to verbalize it, but the fragrance is there and they just know it!

That fragrance, climate, or ambiance may be described in different ways:

- Cheerful or sad
- Healthy or unhealthy
- Encouraging or discouraging
- Optimistic or pessimistic
- Upbeat or downbeat
- Go for it or hold back

What Think Ye?

- Stretch and grow or don't rock the boat
- Challenge the status quo or don't change anything
- Dream the dream and do it or sleep on it another day

Whether you say it or not, the ambiance is there. In a healthy climate, there will be positive, high energy-level performance. Relationships will be authentic and vibrant. People will feel fulfilled in what they do. They will enjoy being in the environment where you are their leader.

How would you diagnose the ambiance in your organization at this moment?

A leader's primary role is climate control. The passive leader who simply permits a "whatever" climate to develop will see mediocrity and often a lack of purpose among his followership.

What think ye?

Climate Control Takes Intentionality

Leaders must be lifelong learners in staff and team leadership development. The Bible, of course, is our primary source, but like Jesus, we can draw learning from everyday life by:

- Constantly reading books on leadership. Always be reading!
- Regularly attending training opportunities available—often. You don't know it all!
- Networking with other leaders via email, phone, or personal conferences.
- Not staying in your own private fortress and watching the world pass by while you think you are living on the cutting edge of life. In reality, your cutting edge might be rather dull.
- Staying fresh and up-to-date on articles related to your areas of expertise, using such resources as *Creator* magazine, *The Choral Journal*, and yes, even *USA Today*!

If you are a leader, make sure you are creating a good climate or ambiance for those who follow you. It will pay great dividends in the future.

What think ye?

Sad versus Happy

I'm sad for those men and women who are really hurting and have been treated unfairly in the process of being asked to leave their positions without due cause.

I'm sad for those who have been released from their church and who, in their hearts, know they really haven't done a good job or kept up with the times and wish to blame someone else for their troubles.

I'm sad for those who have been released from their church for no reason other than a new pastor coming on board and his desire to bring his own staff, and the congregation accepts this kind of leadership without question.

I'm sad for the churches that allow this kind of treatment to continue without investigation and resolve of the issue.

I'm sad for staff members who are leaving and really don't realize that the pastor is the spiritual leader of the church and therefore, they, as staff members, are under God to allow him this leadership. If the pastor, through his ministry in the church, is maintaining moral, ethical, and doctrinal purity as called for in Titus 1:5–9, then staff members are under his leadership. As Walter Cronkite used to say, "And that's the way it is."

I bless God for every church leader who is . . .

- Happy in their church and calling from the Father
- Blessing God for the opportunity to be in His vineyard
- Serving faithfully and aggressively to lead in the twenty-first century
- Ministering outside church lines
- Sharing the good news of the Gospel of Jesus Christ through the avenue of service to others
- Loving and encouraging those who come weekly to sing the praises of God
- Studying God's Word faithfully and sharing the overflow with the others
- Keeping him/herself up-to-date with the many changes taking place in our world.

What think ye?

What Think Ye?

Write It Down!

Frank Tyer once noted, "Success is often just an idea away."

Fresh ideas are the lifeblood of any organization. How readily one acts on those ideas with great potential will often determine the rate and level of their success. If you can see that an idea will improve you, your people, or your organization, it's worth your time to implement it as soon as possible.

Following these five steps will help ensure that a great idea won't die on the vine.

1. Write it down. Stephen Douglas said, "Most ideas are lost if they're not written down within ten seconds." As with any important task, when you take the time to write it down, you decrease the possibility of forgetting it. Make sure that you describe the idea well enough to capture its essence, so when it's time to move forward, you don't need to reinvent it. Tip: Put paper and pens in strategic places so that you will have something on hand to write down your idea.

2. Involve others. Having competent colleagues confirm the value of an idea often provides the added incentive that's needed to move forward. Encouragement is one of the most powerful motivators of action. Also, in the process of sharing an idea, you may discover one better than the original. Tip: Make a list of three to four people whose opinion you value. Make sure that you have spoken to each before implementing an important decision.

3. Set a deadline and stick to it. Once you've determined that an idea is valuable, set a deadline to implement it. This will encourage action and provides accountability within the organization. Tip: In order to effectively set time lines, you will need to become an expert in prioritizing.

4. Let go of your preconceptions. Don't wait until everything is "perfect" to begin implementing a great idea. That time will never come. You'll be stuck in the land of waiting forever. Instead, throw out those preconceived notions of what can or cannot be done, and determine to set a new precedent in your thinking. Tip: Thinking "outside the box" is difficult for many people. Work on your presentation. Be positive.

5. Just do it. It's often much easier to act your way into thinking than to think you way into acting. The more time you spend acting on great ideas, the sooner you'll increase your organization's potential for success. Great ideas need landing gear as well as wings. Tip: Break your idea into a step-by-step plan to make it more manageable, and start the first step today!

Great ideas have a short shelf life. You have to act on them before the expiration date. Benjamin Franklin said, "To succeed, jump as quickly at opportunities as you do to conclusions." Make a commitment today to begin jumping at great ideas, rather than analyzing them to death, because the greatest brainstorm in the world is worthless if you can't find a way to harness it.

We sure need more great ideas today. Will your idea be the next great one?

What think ye?

Want to Know a Secret?

A great secret of great success for leaders is to be able to dream dreams about your leadership that are completely and utterly unrealistic!

Go beyond the dream. Try to create things in your program that are totally unreasonable, unrealistic and even absurd! Such a dream requires an obsession that is worthy of your highest and your best effort! It requires going beyond the ordinary. Unusual success in ministry of any size requires seeing something bigger, something beyond what others can see.

Never fear your "impossible" dream! Embrace it! Each is a script from which you create a program you and God really want.

Walt Disney once made this challenging comment: "If you can dream it, you can achieve it."

Leaders must work extra hard to achieve their ministry dreams! Dreaming "the dream" involves searching and finding creative people to help in the process and the program to make it a success. It can be done!

Dream it!
Do it!

What think ye?

What Think Ye?

Are You a Reader?

If you are not a reader, then maybe you are not a leader! There is so much out there. Is that the reason—that there is so much out there? I love to read. I really enjoy the Clive Cussler, Stuart Woods and James Patterson books. These are good "plane trip," down time, or travel reading times for me. I also like to read articles and books on leadership and development. I recently received a new Kindle. It is such a great tool for reading!

"How can I read when I do not have any time left in my day?" you ask. Simple! You find the time!

- Read early in the morning, following your devotions.
- Read late at night, after you have enjoyed supper with your precious family and have relaxed a bit.
- Read a chapter or two before you turn out the light.
- Read on weekends or on your day off. You do take a day off, don't you?

In today's fast-paced world, the person who reads and keeps up with what is going on in the world, developments in leadership, changes in society and tips on self improvement will be the one who will be well-prepared for whatever comes his way.

I saw a T-shirt recently that had on the front: "I read. Therefore, I think."

On the back, it said: "I think. Therefore, I read."

What think ye?

The Joy Factor

If a leader is to have the joy factor in his life and ministry, it will require the following things:

1. Adequate attention to your personal walk with the Lord. This is a basic, a must, an obvious part of effective spiritual leadership. Without it, we are only kidding ourselves about our effectiveness as leaders. How long has it been since you had a regular, daily devotional time alone with God? How long has it been since you and

Personal Attitude

your spouse prayed together? How long has it been since you had a message from God? How long, O Lord, how long?

2. Constant evaluation of your real motive for leadership. Why do you do what you do? Can you recall your calling, or has this been long-ago forgotten and you are now running on personal motivation rather than inspired motivation by the Holy Spirit? When was the last time you actually evaluated your personal leadership skills?

3. Proper balance between work and leisure. Some people think work and fun are separate, never together in the same job description. How sad. Many leaders have no sense of humor in the workplace and expect their followers to be the same way. Much of life is laughable, full of humor, and much of it happens in the workplace daily! Allow a bit of fun to enter into your work ,and you'll enjoy your work more because you will be having fun doing it!

4. Attention to growth as a person, family member, church leader and community citizen.

   For instance:

   - When was the last time you attended a PTA meeting with your child?
   - When was the last time you attended a stimulating conference that increased your own personal leadership skills?
   - When was the last time you voted in an election?
   - When was the last time you accomplished something that you felt contributed to the well-being of your neighborhood or community?

All four of these areas are critical to effective ministry! I am especially concerned that so many of ministers center on their own local church and never get outside those walls for professional or spiritual growth.

So, how do these leaders grow musically, spiritually, socially and emotionally?

Here comes a penetrating question: When was the last time you specifically led your followers to grow spiritually, musically, socially and emotionally?

Wow! Heavy questions here!

What think ye?

What Think Ye?

Habits

Everyone has them. Everyone is familiar with them. Habits can make us stronger, more disciplined and worthy of the task to which we have been called, or habits can weaken our character, harm our influence and cause a poor reflection on God's Kingdom that lives within each of us.

I have a daily habit I really enjoy. I rise around 7:00 a.m., pick up the papers, pour a good cup of strong coffee and prepare a muffin; then I sit in my chair to read the local news and *USAToday*. After that, I read several devotional books and then, pray for my family and God's Kingdom. It is a good habit. It gets me off on the right foot.

When I was in the local church, and later, when I was teaching university-level freshmen music theory, I had to work hard not to develop habits that would make my life much easier and not cause me to work quite so hard. These would be things such as using the same worship template week-after-week and simply filling in the blanks for the coming worship experience—or to rely on last year's assignments and tests for my frightened freshmen. It would have been so easy to do either of these. But something in the back of my head would always pierce my being and remind me that creativity, new energy and working a bit harder to please the Father—as well as my pastor and later my dean—should be foremost in my planning.

You and I know people who shortcut worship planning and have gotten into the habit of shortchanging the people of God by not spending time planning creative and innovative worship experience and working through the maze.

You and I also know men and women who agonize weekly over the worship service planning, ensuring that a fresh worship experience will take place each Sunday and help the people come before God's throne and experience true worship.

There are some very fine church music habits that are good ones and should be used effectively. Among these are ten quality habits:

1. Always beginning and ending rehearsals on time.
2. Always beginning the worship experience on time and leaving it open-ended for the Spirit of God to work among His people.
3. Never singing with the choir! They don't need you and probably wish you wouldn't do it!

4. Doing everything yourself in an attempt to become the super minister of music or worship leader, thinking that the more you do, the more your people will appreciate you. Sorry! It doesn't work that way.
5. Being willing to go "out of your way, on your way" to be an effective minister to your people.
6. Spending quality and quantity time with your family, giving them some of your best times.
7. Always challenging your people to stretch themselves to be better than they are and complimenting them often in the process.
8. Being able to laugh at yourself and not be uptight over the little things in rehearsals, with staff, or in worship. Unprepared funny things do happen. Relax and enjoy the moment.
9. Giving credit where credit is due, always taking the last bow, and showering praise and affection upon those who do so much in your ministry program. You cannot appreciate people too much.
10. Spending quality time in the presence of the One who called you into your ministry, gaining instruction and lessons for the coming days.

Habits. We all have them. Make sure to keep the good ones and dismiss the not-so-good ones!

What think ye?

Where Do You Go to "Fill Up"?

When your car gets close to being empty, you pull into a service station and . . . "fill up!"

When your fridge gets low on food items, you go to the grocery story and. . . ."fill up!"

When your tires get low on air, you pull in, go to the air machine, and . . ."fill up!"

When you get low spiritually, and/or emotionally, where do you go to "fill up"? Does it surprise you that many choose not "fill up" on a regular basis?

What Think Ye?

As leaders, we just keep giving and giving and giving and giving, even though we are running on "empty," and we think "they" don't know that we are "running on empty!"

Boy, are we wrong! We can only give and give and give so much before we have to be refilled, renewed, revived and restored, so that we can be fresh, inspired and able to give again.

So, where do you go for your leadership and spiritual "fill-up"? Every team member needs a "fill-up" at least five or six times a year. Anything less is unacceptable to your spiritual and leadership well-being.

Where can you go to get one of these "fill-ups"?

Almost every area of leadership expertise has a series of summer workshops, where there are many renewal classes that will give you a different perspective on life and leadership skills. You should make reservations soon! So get involved and be prepared to refill! Try the Willow Creek Leadership Conferences in August of each year. This is perhaps one of the best around.

Do something! Get yourself renewed in your leadership skills and style.

So . . . where do you go to "fill-up"?

What think ye?

Words

The Lord and Father gave each of us a tongue, mouth and lips to speak to and communicate with each other and with Him. Positive and reinforcing conversation can be an oasis in the desert of a dreary day!

Who needs this kind of conversation?

- Your children. How long has it been since you praised and complimented one of your children for something done well? If it has been more than a day, that is too long!

- Your spouse. Sometimes, just the right word of praise can make the day for us! "Thank you for the fresh coffee." "I so appreciate you mending my pants!" "You were so gracious to wash all the clothing and put things in the right drawers." It is the little things that really count! Take nothing for granted.

- Your co-workers. Your secretary or boss or even the one who opens the doors could use a word of praise today. A simple: "Good morning, .how is your day going? Thank you for always _____!" This will make them smile—guaranteed!
- The grocery checker. My mom used to check groceries at the local store in my Virginia hometown. She told me once that she could count on the fingers of one hand how many times people ever said a kind word to her! Shame on us. We have many kind words to give away. Let's use some.

Plan this week to spew forth positive and reinforcing words to those whom you meet and influence. You will be amazed at the response from all with whom you come in contact. You will make their day!

What think ye?

Character

Character is built very slowly, generally over a lifetime. The character of a person is hewn, shaped and molded from life experience—those times that are good and those that are not-so-good. The way we respond to the experiences of life will determine the kind of character we are building.

In everyday life, things will not go as planned. Everything will not always "come up roses." Life has little surprises, causing our character to be put to the fire.

Character is a bit like a good credit rating. It can go bad rather quickly. Those of us in ministry should always be on the lookout for things that will corrupt or damage our character. According to 1 Corinthians 15:33: "Bad company corrupts good morals."

This has never been truer than today! Henry Blackaby said recently that the greatest sin among ministers today is pornography. What are ministers thinking when they go online and involve themselves in such activity? What are they thinking when they do anything that is contrary to their sacred calling in Christ Jesus?

Or, are they thinking at all? Probably not! Have they even thought about the effect on their families if and when they get caught? (And they will get caught—if not here, certainly "there"!) Has the "Jesus gift"

What Think Ye?

departed their spirits, and are they controlled now by the powers of evil? I urge you, dear brothers and sisters to stay true to your calling. Continue to build your character so that when people see you, are involved with you in ministry, or work with you, they can say, "This is a man/woman of great character!"

What think ye?

Dignity

Dignity. The very word rolls off the tongue and the head slightly moves in saying the word. Try speaking it. See, your head did slightly move! Dignity is a stately word, calling to mind, at least, to me: greatness, gentleness, authority, character, leadership, respect, stately, regal, confidence and spiritual depth.

In a conversation with a friend recently, he said these words to me: "There isn't much dignity left these days in worship, is there?" His words caught me off guard. This friend is a faithful church attendee. He not only attends his own church but also, because of his job has opportunity to visit churches of all denominations and worship services of all styles across the country, so his words were not off-the-cuff words. They were heart words.

I began to think about dignity and how it applies to a worship experience, and I must now confess to you that my friend is probably correct in his wording. As a believer, committed to my Lord and Master, and after trying to be a faithful servant for many years, I think I know, at least in my own mind and for me personally, what true worship should be and what the act of true worship entails. "Worship the Lord in the splendor of his holiness." (1 Chronicles 16:29) This is certainly a good place to begin!

How I worship God involves so many different characteristics but includes such things as:

- Creativity, done with beauty and grace
- Scripture, read with authority and meaning
- Sermons, relevant to my daily living
- Music: choral, instrumental, keyboard, handbells, children, adults, youth, ensembles, and of course, congregational singing

- Everything prepared and presented in good taste, no matter the style

In other words, my personal worship includes as much dignity as possible. Haphazard or on-the-spot worship planning is an affront to Holy God. Off-the-cuff worship is as distasteful to the Holy One as it is to the people who have to suffer through it.

Don't misunderstand here. I'm not suggesting that my worship experience is formal, stiff, uptight and strained. Far from it. I was recently a part of worship in a wonderful church, and it was obvious to all that the staff takes the worship experience very seriously. Yes, there is dignity and a printed order-of-worship, but often, a bit of creativity from the Holy Spirit crept in and surprised everyone. The service had the following elements:

- Handbells
- Brass choir
- Organ
- Piano
- Two hymns
- Two choruses
- Scripture read as a congregation
- Two anthems
- Two prayers
- The Doxology
- A vocal duet on the names of Jesus in every book in the Bible, with PowerPoint
- Pledge to the Bible

And all of this in exactly 65 minutes! There was something in this worship experience for every one of every age and walk of life!

I have a firm conviction that every aspect of the worship experience should be "done in a fitting and orderly way" (1 Corinthians 14:40).

That is the part I think is missing today in many churches and certainly, in the worship planning. Since worship is sacred, God-honoring, holy, and we are allowed to approach the throne of the Almighty and

What Think Ye?

bathe in the glory of His presence, to be transformed and conformed to what He wants us to be in the vineyard where He has planted us, it seems to me that there should be some awe or mystery somewhere in the worship process. Psalm 111:10 says: "The fear of the Lord . . . is the beginning of wisdom." I fear that we don't fear the Lord enough in worship. Fear, awe, mystery, conviction, change, repentance and, of course, dignity should all be a part of worship.

Worship is more than:

- Singing loud and fast
- Singing everything in unison
- Music: choral, etc.
- Clever choreography
- Color-coordinated outfits or robes
- Spotlights, cameras and action
- Shallow texts to dreadfully repetitive music
- Hymn texts that speak to another generation long since past
- Me in the forefront, rather than Him
- Hymns and anthems led and sung without joy
- Excitement, music discipline and energy
- Sermons emphasizing only evangelism to a congregation of mostly saved people
- Being compelled to stand for long periods of time
- Clapping and yelling, or faces with sad expressions
- Announcements spoon-fed to the people, interrupting the flow of worship
- Fellowship time, which disrupts the worship mood and flow

When I pass from this earth and go into the presence of the Holy God and see Jesus standing at the right hand of the Father, and with all the Saints and Stalwarts of the faith standing around the Throne, I doubt I will want to go into His presence with anything but fear, awe and realization of my public, personal and private sins. I doubt I will want to do much shouting, hand-clapping or jumping around. I do believe that I will be struck by the overwhelming presence of God Himself, seated on His throne, looking me straight in the eye, reaching for me with outstretched hands, and hopefully, saying to me: "Well done, good and faithful servant."

Remember: the way you choose to worship says more about you than about the worship experience. God loves all worship that is from the heart, worship that honors Him, lifts up His Son Jesus, and transcends us from the norm to the sublime. I can't help but think that dignity plays a very important role here.

What think ye?

Choices

We are in the process of choosing something almost everyday of our lives.

We choose certain fruits to eat. We choose which section of the paper to read first. We choose whether to read and pray today. We choose whether or not to compliment/affirm spouse and children.

We do our choosing with such randomness, without even thinking about it most of the time. If it were true , as J.K. Rowling wrote, "It is our choices that show what we truly are, far more than our abilities," then it would seem to me that we would become very choosy with our choices so that our would most benefit our Redeemer and our families.

Every one of us has made a stupid choice at one time or the other; it is those life-changing, life-altering choices that can get us into the most trouble! Choices such as being faithful to your spouse beyond a shadow of doubt; caring, loving, affirming and protecting your children; and giving careful attention to your job and to your employer are the ones that are life-changing.

Being honest in all dealings are the choices that can be the most life-changing. Far too many brothers and sisters have made wrong choices, and are paying the consequences for it. Be wise, dear ones, in your choices.

Character should take dominion over ambition and personal satisfaction!

What think ye?

What Think Ye?

A Zeal He Does Not Own

There is a wonderful, thought-provoking text by the hymn writer, Frederick W. Faber (1814–1863), entitled "There's a Wideness in God's Mercy," and it speaks to this generation perhaps even more powerfully than to his generation. It is not sung as often as it should be these days, and this is a tragedy for it speaks great truth that we should be hearing and singing in times like this.

You may remember the first stanza:

> "There's a wideness in God's mercy
> Like the wideness of the sea
> There is kindness in His justice
> Which is more than liberty."

This is pretty heady stuff! Read it again carefully, and see if the Holy Spirit brings some fresh thoughts to your mind. It certainly did to me. I'm prone to think about justice and liberty not only as it relates to our country, but also to the church. God, in His tender mercy and grace, has great kindness in His justice and liberty, and He doesn't desire to see these characteristics trampled by people who think, in their position, have the freedom to disregard this mercy, kindness, justice and liberty in favor of their own agenda.

Now here is the third stanza, often omitted from many hymnals:

> "But we make His love too narrow
> By false limits of our own
> And we magnify His strictness
> With a zeal He does not own."

I fear this stanza might be left out of some hymnals on purpose. The message may be entirely too close to what is going on in churches today, and it might not be good for people to sing this stanza, be allowed to think on their on and be reminded that some of the things that are happening are from "a zeal He does not own."

I don't have to list these over-zealous actions or false limits because you are already thinking of those that are affecting your life even as you read this. I also do not need to list specifics for they are too many and too varied. If Jesus were involved, He would not want to be part of such "narrow love," our own "false limits," and seeing us magnify His strictness with a zeal He does not own."

Perhaps, if we began to include all five stanzas of this great hymn regularly in our worship experiences, we might begin to see our congregational leadership begin to take a fresh look at this "zeal" and see who really owns it.

What think ye?

Don't Make It—Fake It

I was reading a very fine magazine last month, and I came across a full-page ad that caught my attention at first glance. It advertized a special food dish. This was the headline in huge letters and fancy print: "Don't Make It—Fake It!"

All I had to do, according to the ad, was purchase this product, follow simple directions, prepare the dish, and present it as if I had actually made it!

I'm all for simple recipes, easy cooking and so forth, but to advertise that one should not make the dish, but buy their product and fake it as their own creation, struck me as sending the error message! What would you say if you prepared such a fake dish and your guests raved, begging for your recipe and asking where you found such a wonderful dish? My guess is that you might be a bit embarrassed and have to admit: "I'm sorry! I faked it!"

I began to think about church music ministry as it relates to this ad and thought of several scenarios that would be interesting for us to consider.

- Don't keep yourself sharp in your ministry. Fake It!
- Don't attend conferences/workshops to keep yourself musically, spiritually and professionally fit. Fake It!
- Don't practice your craft. Fake It!
- Don't plan worship ahead of time. Fake It!
- Don't spend time with the Father who called you into His service. Fake It!
- Don't prepare a rehearsal plan. Fake It!

What Think Ye?

- Don't plan on getting a good music education to make you a more qualified music ministry leader. Fake It!
- Don't study your rehearsal music. Fake It!

I'm sure you could come up with some good thoughts on this subject, too!

Having been in the church music scene since 1956, I've been around almost every music ministry corner. I have experienced fellowship, worship, inspiration, challenge and leadership from many, many men and women who would never in a thousand years consider faking it! It would be a moral crisis for them to even consider such an act.

And, I've had time with people who make an obvious practice of faking it—in worship, in rehearsals, in education and in ministry. This has always saddened me.

I thank God for those out in the music ministry trenches who never fake it but lead with professionalism, seek to polish their craft, stay up-to-date, know the music before rehearsals, and always look for something that will challenge their people and themselves in process.

"Don't Make It—Fake It!" This is a misleading statement to those of us who care that the "lamp of excellence" is slowly diminishing!

What think ye?

Fellowship of the Saints

I've been noticing something the past few months that might cause us to do some thinking on the fellowship of the believers (and non-believers) in worship services. Seems it can't be all that difficult to create some time for church members to fellowship, really fellowship, with each other week after week!

Here is what I've noticed:

The one-on-one fellowship, shaking hands, hugging, having just plain old good time with other church members seems to usually happen better at contemporary services than traditional services.

Wait! Don't judge me yet!

Why is this? What causes this? What are the reasons that contribute to this phenomenon?

Personal Attitude

- Since the contemporary services are usually more casual, people seem to be more at ease and actually seek out friends for a visit.
- There are no pews in most contemporary services, which allows people access to each other without the hindrance of immovable pews.
- The contemporary crowd is usually younger in age than most traditional services. Younger people do not mind getting up and walking over to a friend and leaving their seats to do so. Sometimes, in traditional services, the pew seat is chosen, and people do not want to give up this seat because it probably has been in the family for decades, and they fear someone might sit there.
- Because a contemporary service is more relaxed in nature and the people seem more free to speak out, raise hands, say "Amen," and agree out loud with and encourage the pastor, this trend spills over into the fellowship time before and after the service. I was recently in a contemporary service that was over at 12:10, and it was almost 12:30 before most of the people begin heading toward the doors. They had been very busy talking, laughing and visiting.

It seems to me that a traditional or traditional/blended service could have this same kind of good fellowship, but it would have to be, to paraphrase a familiar lyric in musical, "South Pacific," "It has to be carefully taught!"

Welcoming people in the beginning, middle or end of the worship experience doesn't work. Sometimes, people don't know the people around them and find it uncomfortable to visit with unknown people, or perhaps don't wish to shake hands with a stranger. Henry Blackaby has said many times, "Welcome of guests and announcements do more to harm the Spirit of God in worship than any other single thing." Wow! What a strong statement.

Perhaps, some creativity could be fostered in all services that would develop a friendly atmosphere.

For instance, one of the best ways to invite friendship has happened in several churches has been to have a free coffee bar in the atrium, narthex or a nearby room before a service begins, where coffee, juice and muffins are available free of charge. People will come for food, and fellowship usually will follow!

What Think Ye?

If fellowship is important to a church, then in this new century, church leaders have to dream, think, plan and execute ways to increase the fellowship of their people, while finding ways to include visitors and non-members.

No one said this would be easy! But I think it is at least worth a discussion in staff meeting or staff retreat!

What think ye?

Music Shapes Us

Recently, I was reading a remarkable book by Susan Palo Cherwien, titled *From Glory Into Glory, Reflections for Worship* (MorningStar Music, $24.95-permission granted). You should read this book! It will fill your heart and mind with thoughts that will challenge you in your ministry.

On page eight, I was completely captured by what Cherwien wrote, and I have permission to share her lines with you:

"Music is benign. Words are not neutral.

Music can pierce us to the heart, shape us, form us.

Words have power- power to ascend—power to throw down.

In the temple of Jerusalem, it was the duty of the high priest to enter the Holy of Holies once each year on the Day of Atonement—Yom Kippur—and speak aloud the Holy Name of God.

Before He entered, the other priests tied a rope to his leg so that, if his heart was impure and he died in the presence of God, the other priests could drag him back out.

Words are not neutral. Words have power. Music is not benign.

Music shapes us—forms us.

Are we singing Holy words? Are we singing Holy songs?

Into what are we being shaped by the words of our mouths?

Should someone tie a rope to our leg?"

One of the awesome, powerful and challenging parts of planning weekly worship is to make sure God's people, young and old, sing texts that have spiritual meaning and melodies that touch the heart and soul. Then, together, this can bring God's people into one holy Body of Christ. It's not an easy task, is it? Is someone trying to tie a rope to your leg? Meditate on and read again and again the words Cherwien wrote. I'm reading them everyday this month.

What think ye?

Planning for Fall and Spring

Planning.

The plan.

Thinking up the plan.

Actually having a plan.

Carrying out the plan.

Allowing others to be a part of the plan.

Wishing you even had a plan!

What is your plan for the Fall? Do you have a Fall plan? Yes, it will be Fall soon. If you have the plan for Fall, you are well on your way. If you have not yet thought about your plan, it is almost too late. Here are some thoughts that might encourage your plan:

1. Have a plan. Create a map for getting your plan accomplished, and put dates with it! If you desire 10 new choir members for the Christmas program, map out plans as to how you will accomplish this. The beauty of a plan is that it allows you to chase and accomplish your dreams and goals.
2. The efficient leader plans and innovates!
   - Planning is a state of mind.
   - Planning gets better as one works at it.
   - Planning provides a context for decision making.
   - Planning creates a framework for decision making.
   - Planning focuses attention on program direction.

What Think Ye?

- Planning builds increased communication and facilitates an approach to problems and decision making which is characterized by comprehensiveness and relevance.
- Planning identifies and weighs the limiting factors.

3. Three steps to develop your plan:

- Decide where you want to go. Most of us make this far too complicated. People assume they have to know every detail about every choice they will ever have to make. Then, since no one can know all that, they decide the process is too hard. That's just silly! If you don't want to plan, just be honest, and don't do it!
- Be honest about the present. Reality never lies, and to reach any goal it's important to know your starting point. That means doing some year-end review. How much have you learned this year? How have you refreshed your ministry skills? What have you truly accomplished this year?
- Create a plan, draw a map. It's not hard, but it does require time and energy. Do you want to improve your ministry skills? Plan to do it. Do you want to be a better leader/conductor? Plan to do it.

Again, this isn't hard, but it does require a plan and the discipline to follow it.

Remember this: most people have no Plan at all. They go from day to day, working very hard, but not necessarily making much progress. Don't let that be you! Decide what you want, get very clear about where you are right now, and then work to close the gap.

The end of the year is a time for reflection, dreams and future planning. It is a time to review your progress, examine your choices, and make new choices and commitments. It's time to plan! You can no longer wait. Ready? Set? Plan!

What think ye?

Personal Attitude

Choose Your Ruts Carefully, and Don't Run out of Gas

A long time ago in Alaska, before paved roads were readily available, there was a sign posted at the beginning of a road that would lead to the next town. The sign read:

"Choose Your Ruts Carefully!

You will be in them for the next 200 miles!"

And at the beginning of a very long bridge from Tampa to St. Petersburg, Fla., there is an eye-catching sign in bold letters that reads:

"It is against the law to run out of gas on this bridge."

These two signs gave me food for thought as I prepared this essay. Allow me to take these separately.

First, "rut-mania" seeps slowly into a ministry routine, and often we don't even realize it. It reminds me of the frog in a pan of cold water sitting on a stove. As the water is gradually heated, the frog is content to sit and enjoy the rising heat until it is too late. Of all the ministries of any local church or of all the programs in schools and colleges, the music ministry program should be the most creative, always innovative, creating interest and showing leadership in such a way as to inspire those who follow. One does not do this by spending the majority of time in the fortress/office behind the desk.

Innovation and creativity happen as one is out and about doing ministry, reading leadership books, searching for new ideas and, of course, looking for good music. Notice I didn't say "new" music. As I have said many times before, music is not necessarily good because it is new.

"Rut-mania" comes slowly when one chooses to do the same music season after season, year after year.

"Rut-mania" comes slowly as one chooses to do everything by him/herself rather than training leadership to help and assist in a wide variety of responsibilities.

"Rut-mania" comes slowly when ministry becomes more show than worship, and thoughts turn to bigger rather than better.

"Rut-mania" comes slowly when worship becomes all about you and less about Him.

"Rut-mania" comes slowly when youth and children's choirs are eliminated or rehearsal time is severely cut.

"Rut-mania" comes slowly and begins to sink in when there are not any trained musicians to fill music leadership positions.

What Think Ye?

But, thank God, we can get out of "rut-mania," and we are not bound to spend our ministries traveling in the ruts. Ruts are never too deep that one can't get out if one really desires to do so! A friend told me recently that a rut and a grave are similar, only the grave is just a bit deeper.

The second sign comes to mind when one tends to run out of gas in ministry because of not taking advantage of conferences and workshops that will refresh one's mind, energy, enthusiasm, spiritual life and ministry ant that will also provide new and creative ideas that can enhance a program and help avoid "rut-mania." Just because one has a college or seminary degree or two doesn't mean one is finished learning. It pains my spirit to talk with young leaders and hear them say they aren't going to graduate or they are not going to graduate school because they already have a good church with a good salary, and their pastor tells them they don't need any further education. How sad! A person who accepts this kind of mindless advice is destined one day to be out of ministry and into another vocation!

Running out of gas can happen often to church staff ministers, for these men and women are always on the giving end of life. If one doesn't take the time to refill the creative spirit tank, one finds it difficult to stay fresh.

How does one refill his creative spirit tank? It is so obvious! This happens naturally as one attends good conferences, workshops, reads leadership books, participates in stimulating conversation with friends and most of all, getting out of the fortress/office and becoming involved with real people! A remarkable and readily available resource is active and continuing friendship with leaders of all denominations in your city and surrounding cities. A once-a-month luncheon with four to five other leadership friends will make for stimulating conversation. Don't say you're too busy! One should never be too busy to improve, renew, learn something new and pray for each other and for each other's ministries.

You don't have to stay in a rut in your ministry.

You don't have to run out of gas in your ministry.

If you feel you are in a rut or have run out of gas, don't be like the frog and just remain content until it's too late. Do something! Go somewhere! Become alive again! Your ministry deserves no less than your best all the time! Anything less is an affront to the God who first called you.

What think ye?

Personal Attitude

Doing More Than Expected in Your Job Description

What an interesting statement!

But if you take time to sit down, be quiet, concentrate and think about what you are doing, you will probably discover that you are doing far more than is expected in your job description.

No way, you say? Well, let's look at some possibilities where you might find yourself guilty of doing way too much.

- How about scheduling 10 to18 Christmas performances instead of the normal two to four? Can you name any church members who have asked, begged, pleaded and/or threatened you to have so many extra performances? Think about what these many performances are doing to the family members of those expected to be involved in these performances. What about time away from the spouse and children, the regular schedules interrupted and much, much more. Not in your job description.

- You are attempting to direct 10 or more choirs, instrumental or vocal ensembles, bell choirs, and praise teams that you could "farm out" to talented people standing in the wings who just need to be invited to help. Ten groups is too much! If you are doing this much and the music ministry falls apart when you leave for greener pastures (if there are such,) you have not been a good music minister! One of the main responsibilities that you have for the church is to train more volunteers to be active in the music ministry by directing ensembles, children's choirs and other groups. In a church where I was a recent member, if the current minister of music were to depart, the music ministry would carry on for at least a year or more because talented, trained and excited volunteers are filling all the directing responsibilities except the adult and youth choirs. Oh yes, the minister of music is the overseer of all that went on, but he did not find it necessary to have to conduct all the groups. Directing ten groups is not in your job description.

- Having assistance with all the music ministry responsibilities may just allow you to be at home perhaps two to three nights a week with your spouse and children. Sometimes, your family may go for two or more weeks without really seeing you, having a good family meal with conversation, family devotional and prayer times, and much more. The stress in a family situation is extremely high anyway. You can't do it all by yourself. That's not in your job description.

Get the point? Ease up a bit. Find some time to consider the five R's: Relax, Renew, Rest, Recommit to family and Realize that you are doing more than is required.

If you stop doing so much and give others the opportunity to help, church members will even know you have stopped doing things that are beyond your job description!

What think ye?

four

Email Etiquette

Email Etiquette

EMAIL IS PERHAPS THE most powerful tool developed for our quick communication in this new century, and to know how to use it effectively becomes increasingly important. Email is the most efficient way for quick and easy communication other than the phone, and email is cheaper. Like a poorly written business letter, a poorly written email can lessen your credibility.

Here are some hints for better email etiquette:

1. Always sign your email message. Sometimes, I receive an important email for a prayer request or big news, but there is no name. I'm left guessing who sent the email, and if I can't find out, I can't answer. Always sign your name.

2. An email message is best communicated by not using colors, images, or cute type styles. I compare many of the messages I receive to sending an important business letter on colored stationary with pictures of cats or butterflies in the margin. Many computers and different servers don't have the fonts and colors required, and the email comes to the person looking bland or *whompy-jawed!* It just isn't professional!

3. People sometimes send emails in all caps. It feels like I'm being yelled at the whole time I'm reading it. Caps mean emphasis. Caps are the email way of yelling.

4. Some emails have poor grammar and punctuation. Even though email is a primary tool for quick communication, it reflects you and your personality, just as much as a business letter. Take an extra moment to check spelling, grammar, and punctuation. Use your spellchecker; if you don't have one, get one.

5. Set up a signature file that is inserted at the end of every email you send. Every email program has a way to set up a brief description of who you are. You'll never forget to sign an email if you have this.

6. Attached files are a primary way for computer viruses to spread because they are designed to attach themselves to outgoing email. Make sure you know from whence a file comes before you send it on to someone else. If you pass along a joke or an inspiring story, take time to erase all the other sources from which it comes. I got a four-line story recently that was seven pages long because of all the addresses of the hundreds who had previously sent the story! People are no longer bothering to read "passed on" materials with lots and lots and lots of previous stuff! If you must pass on a story, simply erase all the other "stuff."

7. When changing your email address, send both the old and the new addresses so one can delete the old and add the new.

8. Check stories and prayer requests before forwarding them. The prayer request about the missionary, David, who is dying in China of intestinal virus, is ten years old. David is well, has been in the states, and is now back on the mission field! But the email is still being sent around. The O'Hair story about the FCC wanting to stop religious broadcasting is 20 years old, and she never did even put that request into the government. And, finally, Bill Gates is not ever going to send you any money for tying his products or for any reason!

   A good rule of thumb: before you forward a prayer request or an emergency email, check it out first to make sure it is current. There are lots of things going round that are simply not valid.

9. Answer email quickly. Usually when people send you an email, they are anxiously awaiting a response. Waiting two to three days is as slow as "snail mail," unless, of course, you are unavailable.

10. Use the "subject line" to tell either who the email is from or what the subject of the email is. This keeps people from guessing who and what.

What think ye?

Avoiding Email Faux Pas

Before sending an email, experts recommend the following:
1. Use the subject line to let the reader know how important the message is and be honest about it.
2. Proofread and spell-check, but beyond that, look for other hang-ups also. Avoid sending an email in "anger," for you will regret it later!
3. Make sure the email has something anyone could read, because it could accidentally end up in the wrong mailbox. A good rule of thumb: Never send an email you wouldn't want your mom, spouse, children, or boss to read.
4. Write a clear and logical note, and make sure your email makes good sense!
5. Get to the point quickly. People don't have time to read materials that are not really important to the purpose of the email.
6. Never forward materials to people that probably won't be interested and always check to see if the story is true before sending to a group of people.
7. When sending to a large group, know how to a send a blind copy so that pages are not wasted on email addresses. This is especially true when forwarding something. Simply copy it and forward it to your list, if you must forward it. Some people do not like their email address available to others.

What think ye?

What Think Ye?

The Ten Commandments of Email

1. Thou shalt include a clear and specific subject line.
2. Thou shalt edit any quoted text down to the minimum thou needest.
3. Thou shalt read thine own message thrice before thou sendest it.
4. Thou shalt ponder how thy recipient might react to thy message.
5. Thou shalt check thy spelling and thy grammar.
6. Thou shalt not curse, flame, spam or use all caps.
7. Thou shalt not forward any chain letter.
8. Thou shalt not use email for any illegal or unethical purpose.
9. Thou shalt not rely on the privacy of email, especially in the workplace.
10. When in doubt, save thy message overnight and reread it in the light of the dawn.

What think ye?

five

Success . . . Is Just Around the Corner!

Success

SUCCESS IS NOT AN accident, a run of luck or a mysterious blessing for a fortunate few. Success is about knowing who you are and doing what you love to do. Success is about creating a space where you have a chance, and then giving everything you have to a world that is eager for your unique contribution.

Success requires great patience and a healthy impatience. It requires a determination to be and do your best, and the humility to learn from the masters. It requires a few core competencies. And it challenges and calls to each of us.

Success requires:

1. Personal integrity. It means living your own life and following your own path. Socrates said, "The unexamined life is not worth living." I'm not sure I'd push it that far, but I do know that until we define ourselves and take control of our lives, success is elusive. Each of us is born with unique skills, aspirations, abilities and blind spots, and until we sort them out and find our own path, life is about survival rather than success. Until you find your own path, life can be hard, hard work!

2. Environmental integrity. Success requires a home and office, friends and family and a financial situation that supports you. Organizing our lives and the space around us is an essential ingredient for lasting success. Successful people have nice offices. Great cooks have nice kitchens. Loving families have game rooms, backyards and minivans

that support family activities. Artists and writers have studios.

Do you have the space to create the life you really want? A core competency of success is the ability to manage your environment. Whatever it takes, success requires surroundings that support you. It's an ecology thing. Humans can survive in almost any environment, but we only flourish when the conditions are right! Clean up your nest!

3. Community contribution. Success is about making a difference in your world. The poet, John Donne observed, "No man (or woman) is an island." We are social creatures, and the more we contribute to the richness and vibrancy of society, the more wealth there is for all of us. It doesn't seem to matter what your unique gifts are. Share them with the community. When you make your contribution in your unique way, and give it in a spirit of building community, amazing things happen. It's the price, and the reward, of great success.

4. Future awareness. The final component of success is the ability to plan for the future. We live in an age of instant gratification and easy credit. "Buy now; pay later, even if you don't need it!" is the norm. And, in my opinion, it's a recipe for failure. Successful people know how to delay gratification. They know that the future is where they will spend the rest of their lives, so they arrange it in advance! They tend to be very patient and very wise. They learn from the mistakes of others. They take the long-term view and are rarely seduced by short-term distractions.

What think ye?

Three Rules for Success

1. Clear blueprints. Numbers, dates, costs and measurements give the focus for peak performance. Success is the result of a well-defined goal, and clear, workable plans for achievement. Spend time designing well! Think about what you want. Talk with experts. Read and take notes. The first principle for success is: Know your outcome!

2. Environmental fitness. Time management is no longer. Time just "is." To achieve success, we must manage ourselves as well as the world

around us. Work to make it easy to reach your goal. Winners have clean offices, the best equipment within a budget and clear schedules. When your environment makes success easy, you'll win every time!

3. Support systems. Fill your life with people who encourage you, and learn from people who have achieved what you want to achieve.

There's an old saying that goes like this: "It's hard to soar with the eagles when you're scratching with turkeys."

Surround yourself with cheerleaders, coaches, mentors, models and team members who are committed to help you succeed.

Remember: success is a team activity. Get a coach or mentor who believes in you and is determined to take you to the top!

What think ye?

Focus!

Many times, the ability to focus is most difficult for all of us! This becomes obvious when we have other interests and responsibilities in our lives, and sometimes the ministry can play "second fiddle" to everything else. The ability to focus becomes increasingly important in situations like this.

Here are some guidelines to help you learn to focus:

- Focus on where you want to go with your life and with your leadership.
- Focus is what you want in your life and in your leadership.
- Focus is what you want to be when you grow up and what you envision for your leadership.
- Focus is not only realizing that complaining and blaming others are not only wastes of time, but also realizing that the more one complains and blames, the more one may find to complain about. This is no way to achieve greatness!
- Focus means simply this: to achieve any goal, assess the current situation, determine exactly where you want to go, and get started.

Now, focus!

What think ye?

What Think Ye?

Successful versus Unsuccessful People

Successful people play by the rules and bend them ever so often.

Unsuccessful people either ignore the rules or don't even know there were any rules!

Successful people have goals and direction in their lives.

Unsuccessful people are more reactive, confused, and run in circles, always chasing something, but rarely making any progress.

Successful people are persistent or determined. There is something they want, and they are terribly stubborn about getting it. Successful people are not always the easiest people to live with!

Unsuccessful people "try" things, experiment and they jump on (and off) every bandwagon that comes down the road.

Successful people work harder, although they don't always know it. They just stay later, think clearer and keep tinkering until they get it right.

Unsuccessful people want "passive income" or look for the easy way, while successful people look for what works.

Successful people have rich personal networks, and they ask for advice from the best people.

Unsuccessful people are more likely to give advice, rarely ask for it themselves, and tend to avoid people who might be able to help.

Successful people seem to be naturally generous and giving. They contribute ideas, time, energy, humor, creativity and money to people around them.

Unsuccessful people are always afraid of being ripped off, and they rarely give or contribute.

Fortunately, it's clear that the traits and attitudes of highly successful people can be learned. As you look at this list, notice that determination or the willingness to work hard, or ask for advice, is not genetically predetermined!

Tony Robbins is fond of saying that "success leaves clues," and that we can learn from highly successful people.

Success . . . Is Just Around the Corner!

Success in life, whether in business or in our personal relationships, is not about being born with it or having it handed down. It's an attitude of humility, a willingness to learn and an eagerness to grow.

Success is about making a contribution, about getting along with people, and about persistence.

Success is available to us all.

What remarkable, extraordinary and amazing things will you do with this wild and wonderful miracle—your one and only life?

What think ye?

Top Five Secrets of Being Happy

Do you remember Bobby McFerrin's big hit song a few years ago: "Don't Worry . . . Be Happy"?

Have you ever noticed people's reactions when a highway is closed because of an accident ahead, or some other unusual event occurs while driving and the traffic is stopped?

Some drivers listen to their radio. A few might be eating or doing makeup. Some seem to be working or reading. Still others might opt for a quick nap. There may also a handful who are clearly agitated and angry. They pace about swearing and are visibly upset.

But most have decided that the best response to this event, which none of us could control, is to be happy about it and relax. Traffic will eventually move again! Abraham Lincoln said: "Most people are about as happy as they make up their minds to be."

The following five tips could increase the happiness factor in your life:

1. Decide to be a happy person. As Lincoln observed, most people—most of the time—can choose how stressed or happy, or how troubled or relaxed, they wish to be. Simply choose to be happy.

2. Watch and read less news. We don't need the stress that both local and national television can bring. It is all about the very worst of humanity. So just don't watch.

What Think Ye?

3. Practice the "attitude of gratitude." We all have much for which to be grateful. Just try thanking the many people who assist us, encourage us, teach us and open doors for us; you'll discover this could take all day!

4. Take time. Dogs can teach us a lot of things, such as loyalty, unconditional love, noticing the sights, sounds, and smells in the yard, and about being relaxed and playing. They can also teach us to eat only when we are hungry, to nap when we need it and to get our ears scratched whenever possible! Perhaps we should "wag more and bark less!"

5. Laugh every day. Hear a joke. Tell a joke. Learn to laugh at yourself. Laugh with your friends and family and co-workers. There are very few medicines as powerful as laughter, and you can't over-dose, although it is addicting!

What think ye?

If at First You Don't Succeed, Try a Different Way

Someone has said that a definition of insanity is doing the same thing over and over and expecting a different outcome. My, how that fits some leadership styles these days! We tend to be creatures of habit. All of us fall into ruts, patterns and traditions. We have familiar, comfortable ways of doing things, and we tend to stick to them, even when they don't seem to be working. This is part of the human experience. Without habits and traditions, life quickly becomes unmanageable!

But when traditions create frustration and failure and we can't or won't change, we set ourselves up for tremendous pain in life. We often see this in ambitious, talented people who never quite fulfill their potential. They want success, and they are willing do whatever it takes! But, something holds them back, and often it's this pattern of doing things do not work over and over again.

There is a law that every action creates a result. When one takes action, one gets an outcome or a result from the efforts. If the efforts are not creating the results desired, the key to success is rarely to try harder or to do it the same way again. We might call that stubbornness!

Watch for the patterns in your ministry that do not work, habits that create pain or frustration in your life, and, when you spot them, fix them! Doing things that don't work, while expecting a magical solution, is a road to frustration, heartache and failure. Do what works!

Highly successful people find solutions.

What think ye?

Motivation: The Big "Mo"

Effective leaders should be effective motivators. A healthy leadership style will blossom when members feel motivated to carry out their tasks. As leaders, we should try to make the work as enjoyable and energizing as possible. This requires the skills of motivation.

Here are some important principles of healthy motivation:

1. The Holy Spirit is the staff member's primary motivator. Encourage each person to give highest priority to a close, personal walk with the Lord.
2. Recognize the difference between motivation and manipulation. Motivation is helping persons develop a "want to" concerning tasks. Manipulation is devious management for one's own selfish advantage.
3. Supervision tactics, such as fear and intimidation, may get temporary results, but not for the long haul. Nurturing and empowering have lasting value.
4. An effective leader recognizes individual personalities and temperaments and is able to integrate the differences for the common good of the situation.
5. The leader must work at creating a sense of togetherness in the work setting. This is no place for favorites!
6. Involve others in the dreaming process. They need to feel ownership of the goals.
7. Create an atmosphere of affirmation—a "high stroke" environment. Acute under-appreciation will create an unhealthy work climate. Make sure the affirmation is genuine.

What Think Ye?

8. Be honest with your "followship." If a person needs help doing the task, the leader should communicate this appropriately.
9. Encourage! Provide for ways for your people to take advantage of personal and professional growth opportunities. Provide funding for this.
10. Avoid the "walk-on-water syndrome" as a leader. People already know the imperfections. Admission of them greatly enhances rather than diminishes one's leadership potential.

Keep "Big Mo" on your side.

What think ye?

Leisure Time

Leisure is a most healthy expression of your consideration of life, health and relationships toward others. There should be a bit of leisure time in almost every moment of daily living. How much time should it take to keep you and your family mentally balanced and caught up in daily living with joy, happiness, self-assurance and a good outlook on life?

Caution: remember what leisure time is for you, whatever it might be, should not be imposed on your mate or family! Just because you like to fish doesn't mean everyone should like to fish, so you become tolerant and flexible and increase your scope of activity to include more time with your family. Many leisure activities are available to you and family. Here are some suggestions:

- Walking. In the early morning or late afternoon, you can involve everyone in your family, especially your dog.
- Biking. Enjoy the scenery, the quiet, and the beauty of nature in your area. Set a good pace, and make it so that everyone can keep up.
- Rollerblading. Are you game?
- Nature trips. You could take your family to nature trails, flower gardens, woods, lakes and a local zoo or petting farm.
- Backyard picnics. Do it up right, as fancy or simple as you wish, but make it a big event.

- Beach/lake/pool excursions. Again, make a big event out of it; make it unusual.
- Saturday "your choice" day. One member of the family gets to choose the event for a full day or a half day, and everyone participates.
- Spring cleaning celebration. Advertise this main even for weeks with notes, banners and posters around the house, and everyone gets involved in a big spring cleaning event. Make sure it is full of fun, surprises and gimmicks, and a lot of work will get done. Start with the garage!
- Car cleaning celebration day. Everyone joins in the celebration of cleaning up all the family cars. Some vacuum; some wash; everyone gets wet; some polish; some buff; some fix and bring refreshments.
- Fruit-picking. Find a place where you can pick your own fruit, and let the younger ones go for it and find out where the fruit comes from other than the grocery shelves!

What think ye?

six

Stress . . . Will Take Its Toll

Stress

STRESS IS A KILLER. Stress can paralyze you. Stress is more than capable of making life miserable for you as well as your family!

Yet, so many church staff members continue to pile on stress after stress and wonder why they are agitated, irritable, short with family and others and seemingly weary much of the time.

Most church staff members—ministers as well as other church employees—are currently doing more than their job description requires and more than the church expects. There seems to be the thought that the more they do, the more they will be appreciated. The more they do, the more positive points they will get in their yearly evaluation. The more they do, the more recognition they will receive from church members for always being there for every event that happens in the church calendar regardless of the time it takes away from their family. The more they do, the more words of praise will come forth from church members. (Forget that one!)

To be perfectly honest, all of the previous statements are wrong. In fact, the more we do above and beyond what is expected of us or in our job description, the more the church will expect from us. And even more importantly, this kind of work ethic—doing more and more when it is not expected of us—will impact the one(s) who will follow in our stead.

I'm not saying we should go by "the law" of our job descriptions and, for instance, not be a helper in other ministries, or spend extra time after choir with a member who needs help, or not be flexible.

What Think Ye?

I know of several church where staff members are either burned out or fast burning out due to pressures they are putting upon themselves and are not in any way part of their current job description! They are doing more and more at the expense of time with spouse and children, and I venture to say the same is true in your church situation.

Is there an answer to this style of leadership? Yes! Simply quit doing, going, and being always present for every event—for the sake of your family. Believe it or not, the church will survive without you being involved or present at every function. You are not expected to be at every function.

I know a church in another state where the pastor requires all ministerial staff to be present for all church functions, but couches it this way: "You don't have to be present for the Saturday night service, but it would be good for you to be there." Now, who, in their right mind, would not go because of this pressure? This is wrong. The minister of music had one night at home and now that is gone because of this added service in which he has no part! This kind of staff pressure is not in the best interest of staff relations and certainly will bring the family into stress and conflict sooner rather than later.

Beloved, life at the church went on before you came and it will go on after you leave. Being present for all church activities or doing much more than is required of you might just have a taste of ego, wouldn't you say?

What think ye?

Stress Reducers

You know it. I know it. Everyone knows it. There is a lot of stress in leadership today. It goes with the territory. The preparations, rehearsals, worship planning, sermons, visitations, and all the extra things that have to happen when something huge is looming in front of us will certainly provide an ample dose of stress. It will happen!

Here are some stress reducers that might work for you:

- Always get a good night's sleep.
- As you prepare the day, pray for spiritual guidance.
- Always eat a good breakfast.
- Prepare for today—the night before.

- Write a love note to someone often.
- Read something funny and inspirational each day.
- Look out the window often.
- Laugh a lot.
- Take a brisk walk with a friend or your spouse.
- Avoid negative people.
- Play racquetball or tennis.
- Count to 100 and wait three days before reacting to a bad situation.
- Go to lunch with a dear friend.
- Cut out caffeine.
- Sing a happy song.
- Quit trying to "fix" things for other people.
- Count your blessings.
- Apologize for a mistake.
- Be more forgiving of others—and yourself.
- Always look your best.
- Never slump. Walk tall and proud.
- Exercise—stretch.
- Give honest praise to someone each day.
- Learn to say, "No." It is a complete sentence!
- Never expect people to read your mind!
- Never procrastinate. Get organized.
- Laugh. Play. Pray.

Lighten up! Stress can be beaten!

What think ye?

What Think Ye?

Ten Things to Learn from Criticism

As you are in leadership or on a church staff, be aware that criticism can and probably will abound. There will be comments such as:

- The music is too loud.
- The music is too soft.
- The sermon was too long.
- The sermon was too short.
- There were too many instruments up there today.
- There were not enough instruments up there today.
- You didn't follow the bulletin this morning.
- Why don't we ever divert from the bulletin?
- Why didn't you do this?
- Why didn't you do that?

But, positive learning experiences can come from criticism. Here are ten things to learn from criticism:

1. Keep your perspective. Keep in mind what God has called you to be and do.
2. Be honest. Ask yourself if the critic is possibly right. If so, change what needs to be changed. Your critic has helped you.
3. Learn from criticism. It's dangerous to think every critic is wrong. God may be saying something to you through this experience. Listen carefully and constructively.
4. Move on if you feel the criticism is unfounded. Never feel you must argue or retaliate.
5. Remember you and your critic are probably pursuing the same goal. Some of the severest critics are good people who want to see the work of God progress as much as you do.
6. Remember that the critic may be expressing unprocessed anger or personal failure.
7. Don't dwell on the negative. Take strength from all the positive people in your life, especially your family.

8. In difficult times, make sure your personal devotional time is sharp and focused. Stay connected in God's Word.
9. Encourage others. When you lift another, you are lifted in the process.
10. Remember that God is your Ultimate Audience of Significance. He has the final word on your efforts in ministry.

Now: develop a Christ-like Spirit and listen to criticism, but don't respond. Take what you feel is good and discard the rest. Get on with your life!

What think ye?

Balance or Burnout

Life can be overwhelming at times, can't it? The demands on our time, energy, emotions and skills can hit us from all sides, and the pendulum of life continues to swing. If we are to retain our effectiveness and be cutting-edge in leadership and ministry, balance is needed, or burnout will surely come.

In the process, our family, ministry and perspective on life will suffer, become distorted and our walk with Jesus will become a habit or a boring daily routine.

How can one know if your life is out of balance? Here are three signs of imbalance:

1. You have difficulty sensing God. You cease to hear God's voice in your life and activity. There is no closeness that once characterized your relationship to God. If you are having trouble hearing God speak, you're in trouble at the very heart of Christian leadership!
2. You begin to feel inadequate, alone, worthless and/or fearful. Self-esteem is affected when your life is out-of-balance. You stop looking at things through the eyes of Jesus and begin to use your own eyes, or worse yet, the eyes of others! A recent survey indicated that 70 percent of religious leaders have a lower self-image now than when they first entered the ministry! Remember: how you see

yourself affects how you relate to family, friends, subordinates and colleagues.

3. You lack joy in your life and ministry. Habit, duty and obligation are the results of the things that once brought you joy and fulfillment. Doing things by rote is much less enjoyable than by choice.

Realize that nothing of value is accomplished apart from the leadership of God in our lives and that our health, family and ministry are more important than programs or schedules! If we could only learn this fact of life!! Cut back today—and build a balance for tomorrow.

What think ye?

Keep Yourself Pure

Church ministry in today's world requires those of us in ministry to have absolute fidelity to spouse and family as well as to the sense of purpose in our calling from God into ministry. Many of our brothers and sisters have failed and are failing in this arena today, and as you would guess, the church tends *to* "shoot their wounded," forgetting that the church is *a* "hospital for sinners and not a haven for saints." It seems easier to get rid of the problem and move on rather than to effectively minister to and redeem the person.

In a recent conference, a psychologist made this statement, which shocked me:

> "People in ministry are aware of the call of God on their lives to go into ministry . . . but when ministry turns sour, they become discouraged or disgusted with the ministry and feel they need to get out, there is nothing in scripture or books that gives them permission to get 'out of ministry.' Therefore, some use pornography and the Internet—even at the office—as tools to subconsciously 'get caught' and therefore, get free of the yoke of the bondage, called 'ministry.'"

Wow! What a sobering thought! A gentleman in church leadership in another state told me that probably 15 percent of the ministers in his state are into and hooked on pornography. Henry Blackaby, in a recent retreat, stated that the major sin of all ministers in the USA today is pornography!

Whoa! What's happening here? What is happening in ministry that so many seem to be going faster and faster down the slippery slope to Hell in a hand basket because they can't control their thirst for sex, or alcohol, or gambling, or illicit affairs—or whatever else is causing this failure in life, ministry and marriage—which might include a subconscious desire to get out of the ministry?

The biggest concern is not so much the church or the divine calling, both of which are very important, but the real victims are the family! There is no way under heaven to measure the damage that is done emotionally to the spouse and children when situations like this occur. The children especially are scarred for life. And the spouse? Will the marriage relationship ever be the same? Without major counseling and help, it is doubtful.

Here is a tip worthy of serious consideration: Never, ever, under any condition, for any reason, flirt with temptation.

Determine now that you will not allow yourself to be in a position to do anything that will disgrace the Lord or discredit you, your church or most importantly, your spouse and your children. It is just not worth it! No one or no thing is worth the pain and damage it will cause. A moment's pleasure is not worth a lifetime of sorrow and pain.

Paul's admonition in Ephesians 4:27 is vital: "Don't give Satan a place in your life."

Don't wait until you are tempted to take a stand against temptation.

First Corinthians 15:33 says it plainly: "Bad company corrupts good morals."

Don't forget that.

What think ye?

Is Your Life at Flood Stage?

I love the water. Esther and I had a good-sized pond in our backyard when we lived in Jacksonville, Fla. We thoroughly enjoyed sitting out in the evenings as we downloaded the day with each other and enjoyed the calmness and beauty of the water. It soothed our minds and inner spirits.

What Think Ye?

But, to be honest, I am also quite afraid of water. It is a powerful force. The pond where we lived had boundaries and could not just go anywhere it wished. Only once in the eight years did the pond almost get out-of-control because too much water had come into the pond and not enough water had gone out quickly enough.

Our lives can be sort of like that, too. We go along doing our own thing, like we've done it for year and years, and before we know it, our lives begin to spill over, causing havoc with family, job, relationships and even our health.

Here are some thoughts that might keep you doing the right thing and keep your life from getting to a flood stage:

1. Do you have a great sense of urgency too often? Do you find that most everything you do seems so very important and absolutely must be done today? If so, you are robbing yourself of precious moments of reflection, quietness and serenity, which never ever come with urgency!

2. Do you seem to overextend yourself often, to the point of physical and emotional exhaustion? I have a friend who goes and goes until he becomes ill, usually with a cold or severe headaches, and then he slows down, even goes to bed for a couple of days. Then, he gets up and goes at it once again. His body is trying to tell him something, but he does not listen. Proper rest and good exercise are key issues in avoiding flood stage living.

3. Do you ever take time to really think about and love on your spouse and children, or are they just "there"? Do you often find yourself with them out of duty? How long has it been since you and your spouse took a long walk and talked about your lives together and separate? When was the last time you and your spouse did something you both enjoy doing together, like going to a movie or shopping or walking? When was the last time you and your children went for ice cream, no schedule, just fun time? If it's been longer than two weeks, you are way behind and need to do it right away, like today.

4. Do you skip meals so you have more time to work? I have a friend who goes to work at 6:30 a.m., works hard through lunch and goes home about 6:30 p.m. That is a 12-hour day! He takes no breaks. His superiors do not place this pressure on him! It is his own

pressure. He is doomed to crash and burn soon! Our bodies can't keep a schedule like that and survive.

5. Do you pass on time with the Father because you are so involved in ministry and doing the work of God? Wait a minute! That's why you are in ministry in the first place—because God has called you there and He wants that time with you regardless of your schedule. Get your priorities right!

Real life, quality life, a wholesome life, the good life are in the living of a full life! Real life is not in working. On your deathbed, you will not say: "I wish I could have had one more hour at my desk." You might say: "I wish I could have had one more hour with my spouse, my children and grandchildren."

What's really important to you? Are you at the flood stage in life? There's no time like the present to get priorities in proper order.

What think ye?

Hurry Sickness

Busy. Quickly. Hurry.

These are words that are becoming more and more descriptive of our lives these days, especially those of us in leadership and ministry. There is no need to describe all the mistakes, misunderstandings and confusion as a result of one being in too much of a hurry. All of us have been there!

Here are five signs of "hurry sickness." (From "Building Church Leaders" (Leadership Resources), 2000 *Christianity Today*) See if any of these hit home. If they do, steps should be taken to curb this sickness before it spreads!

1. Speeding up your life. Do you always have the nagging feeling that you don't have enough time to do what needs to be done? Are you one who chafes when you have to wait in a grocery checkout line, you spend a second longer at a stop light, people seem to be in your way on the street or even in the church aisles, your child isn't brushing his teeth fast enough, or your accompanist can't find where you wish to begin rehearsal fast enough? Speeding up your life will only give you more time to chafe! Do you need to be under that kind of added pressure?

2. Multi-tasking. Psychologists call this "polyphasic activity" or doing-more-than-one-thing-at-a-time. People who have hurry-sickness may drive, eat, shave, comb hair, put on make-up, and even do business while talking on the cell phone (which is against the law in most states)—and much of this at the same time. Not only is this dangerous to your health and to the safety of others, it is just not the time to have hurry sickness. There is a place, perhaps, for multi-tasking, but if it is to only speed up your life, it is probably out of place.

3. Clutter. Take a look at your desk. A recent study shows that the average worker has 36 hours worth of work on the desk at one time and spends 3 hours a week sorting through it! Someone said, "A cluttered desk is the sign of a creative mind." I don't like someone moving my desk stuff, for then, I can't find it! We clutter as we speed up our lives. Right?

4. Sunset-fatigue. We come home after work, and those dearest to us end up getting the leftovers of our lives, energy and spirit. Perhaps we are often irritable with spouse and children, the ones who mean the most to us. We promise things will get better in a month or two, but that never seems to happen. We find ourselves staying longer at the church, or watching too much television or scanning inappropriate websites. Sunset fatigue can be overcome! But it will take some work, concentration and a real effort to slow down your life to the point that when you arrive home, you are willing to give your family some of your best time and energy. They deserve it.

5. Love impairment. This is important. Read carefully. The most serious sign of hurry sickness is a diminished capacity to love. Love takes time, and that's the one thing people with hurry sickness don't have. When we get hurried, people become a nuisance. When we get hurried, we start thinking about people in strictly utilitarian terms. We use them instead of loving them. This concept is especially true in ministry. When people, even our family, become a nuisance to us, then we have hurry sickness in its final stages.

Well, do you have or do you have the early signs of hurry sickness? You can change! It's not too late.

What think ye?

seven

Ten Leadership Mantras for Success

Mantra Number One

The two best-kept secrets of leadership, according to Andy Stanley, are: (1) The less you do, the more you accomplish and (2) The less you do, the more you enable others to accomplish.

EVERY LEADER HAS WHAT is called core competencies—those areas in which the leader is very good! Some leaders are good communicators, but poor managers. Some may be good vision casters, but poor on follow-up. Leaders waste valuable time trying to be a better manager when he should stay with his communication skills! The key words might be summed up as: only do what only you can do well.

Almost every leader I have ever known, at some time in their lives, made great attempts at trying to please all of the people all of the time, and it just doesn't work that way! Every leader has been assigned or called to do certain things. What is success for your position?

Allow me get even more personal.

Of the things that define success for you, which of those are in line with your giftedness, the areas where you must focus your attention and energies? These are the areas in which you will excel. Success within that realm of your giftedness has the potential to make you an indispensable leader. Best of all, you will enjoy more of what you are doing in your job assignment!

The moment a leader steps away from his core competencies, his effectiveness as a leader diminishes. And, the effectiveness of every other leader in the organization also suffers. Over a period of time, a leader who is not leading from his best zones will create an unfavorable environment for other leaders in the organization.

Leaders want to make the right impression, especially in the early years, and think only they can do a certain task right.

But leadership is not always about getting things done right.

Leadership is about getting things done well—through other people!

We miss the opportunity to play to our strengths because we haven't figured out that great leaders work through other leaders, who work through other people.

Leadership is about multiplying our efforts, which automatically multiplies our results.

Mantra Number Two

The tendency of the masses is toward mediocrity.

Among the ten mantras for successful leadership, perhaps the most obvious is this above statement. It is more true today than ever before! It has been estimated that perhaps as much as 80 percent of the membership of any church would be sufficiently satisfied if the staff never presented a challenge to do anything beyond the status quo, never rocked the boat, never offered a new and fresh adventure/challenge in Christian growth, and never attempted a new musical or choral work that would stretch both conductor and choir. They are happy and content in their own little world of "that's just the way we to do it."

We can see it in our culture today. We are finding ourselves satisfied with the way things are and wondering why things are not changing as we had hoped. We tend to go with the flow and in the process of leaning toward doing the same old thing, and all of a sudden, we are on the road to mediocrity, the boon of complacency and comfort. We are perhaps finding ourselves:

- Enjoying not having to dream the dream
- Not thinking about the future as much as we used to
- Willing to go along with the flow and enjoying the peace and quiet
- Not having to attend conferences and workshops
- Delaying plans that were once considered important

- Turning the anthem or sermon barrel over and beginning again, without new study or preparation
- Noticing that the people are now leaving the church and the church seems to be on the road to the past rather than to the future.

The dictionary defines mediocrity as "the state of being moderate."

When I was teaching freshmen music theory at Samford University, Birmingham, Ala., I would tell my students on the first day of class: "If you are a composition major, you will make an A in this class because all the rest of your music courses are built on music theory. If you are a music major, you will make a B in this class because every course you take from now on will have it's base built on music theory. If you make a mid-term C in this class, make an appointment with me to discuss a change of majors."

Harsh, you say? Not really! In case you are wondering, the grade of C is moderate, mediocre, average, and God knows, we have too much average in our world today!

Consider this: Would you have eye surgery under a doctor who made C's in graduate school? Would you send your precious child to a doctor who made C's in Medical school? Would you send your wife to a physician who came away with C's in medical school? Of course not! You desire only the best qualified, most talented and most knowledgeable people to care for you and your family . . . and certainly, not anyone with grades of C.

Why, then, should it be different in the church? Why should we allow the church to run on a half-full tank of inspiration and creativity? Why should church leadership be bound by a vocal few who want the commitment to the status quo to remain solid and firm, as the world is ever-changing and moving toward the future?

As leaders, we should not let this happen. An old proverb says, "A rolling stone gathers no moss." Sadly, many of today's churches are moss-ridden because they have not moved in years.

As leaders, we do not have to be satisfied with mediocrity. It is up to the leadership to keep the church ship in the right channel, moving toward creativity, energy, freedom, grace, love, mercy and celebration.

If mediocrity wins, we lose!

What Think Ye?

Mantra Number Three

Have the courage to say "No." "No" is a complete sentence!

Jesus tells us to let our "Yes'" be "Yes" and our "No" be "No." Have you ever said "Yes" and later, regretted saying it? You are not alone! This has happened to everyone, believe me!

Food for thought: "No" is—within this one small word—a complete sentence. Try saying the "No" word in a situation, and as difficult as it might be, you will feel good having said it; at the same time, have a sense of *urgency*.

Why urgency? Simply because of these three reasons:

1. Leadership people seem to be born with a great desire to be people-pleasers and try to please all of the people all of the time, if at all possible. If the "No" word is spoken to a church member's request, it might be taken wrong and cause some problems. From personal experience: I've been there, done that and got the T-shirt!

2. Leadership people have the desire to be of service and be helpful to any and all requests and often sacrifice their own personal or family time to say "Yes," when "No" would be the desired answer. Being of service is a good thing, until it interferes with your personal life, which includes spouse, children, and time spent away from them. Nowhere in your job description does it say these words: "You are required to or even expected to say "Yes" to all requests by church members!"

3. Leadership people tend to be fearful that if they say "No" to certain requests, the opportunity might not come their way a second time. Again, I've been there. If they ask you once, they will probably ask again on a different day for a different reason and in a different situation.

No one should expect leadership people to be at their beck-and-call. Neither should leadership be expected to fulfill every request asked of them! To fulfill all requests would mean working many additional hours a week and miss great family time in the process.

Some people are "users." Know any by name? They use people, abuse people with words sometimes by expecting them to be their personal "go-fers." How sad. It is even sadder that people give in to these people and regret doing it later on!

"No" is a complete sentence! So, let's all say it together:

"No!" Very good! Now, once more with feeling: "No!"

Now, that wasn't so difficult, was it? Carry on.

Mantra Number Four

*The higher you are in the leadership chain,
the less truth you will hear.*

This statement is perhaps the most true of the ten mantras and also the least understood or recognized! Pastors, CEOs, music ministers, university deans, committee chairpersons—anyone who is a position of leadership often never even think about the fact that what they hear most from those who are under their leadership are words of praise and sentences that soothe the mind and/or feed the ego. Rarely, ever so rarely do these leaders hear profound truth.

Why?

Simple. Upper-echelon leaders are too high up the power chain and employees, church members, students, faculty, choir/orchestra members and staff do not wish to rock the boat, get themselves in trouble, offend, or risk telling the truth about one or more situations that possibly could help the leader do a better job or fix a problem.

Who's going to be brave enough to tell the new pastor that he needs to be more open to his congregation or that he is moving too fast with change or he is too heavy-handed in his leadership skills?

Who's going to have the nerve to tell the professor that the always-closed office door does not invite faculty or students to feel the freedom to stop in for advice, counsel or comment?

Who will dare tell the CEO that his leadership style often offends people, or that his humor is degrading, or his comments to co-workers in public borders on abuse?

Who is going to step forward to tell the minister of music that he is singing too loud and should listen more, or that his conducting patterns are not clear, or that he should not keep his head in his music and ignore the choir or orchestra, or can't we ever sing anything new and do it well?

What Think Ye?

You already know the answer to all these questions! No one, or at least, very few, will take the chance for fear of punishment, retaliation, embarrassment or isolation.

The wise leader should take every opportunity to improve and hone his leadership skills, but more importantly, to begin to be a listener to those below him on the leadership chain. He will begin to find out information that will help him do a better job in his position.

Remember: it is always easier to lead with a closed mind than to lead with an open and receptive heart.

Mantra Number Five

When the horse is dead, dismount. (Ken Blanchard)

Of the ten leadership mantras for success, this is my favorite! Blanchard's statement is so typical of organizations, churches and schools that continue doing and promoting programs that have failed, are failing or are destined to fail soon. It fits almost everyone who is in a leadership position and thinks they can continue to do the same old thing, change the name and no one will notice.

How wrong is that? Of course, people will notice! Certainly people will ask this question in their minds, if not publicly: "Haven't we done that before, and didn't it fail ?So why are we doing it again, with a different name?"

Reasons for not dismounting the dead horse include:

1. It is easier to stay on the dead horse than to get off! Getting off even a dead horse requires effort. It requires flexibility. It requires thinking. It requires movement. It may even require extra work!

2. To dismount the dead horse means failure! Wrong! Dismounting the dead horse (program) simply means a new direction is necessary. It will require creative thinking, movement and work, but it will be a new challenge for leadership and people to dream a new dream, to explore a new adventure and "to go where no organization, school or church has ever gone before!"

3. The dead horse has been around for years. Some people will say: "It worked before, so why can't it work now?" A church program

that is based on the 1950s/1960s/1970s style of church will not make it in the twenty-first century! The most difficult thing any church will do is "to get off a dead horse" (failing program) and let it go! Church today is vastly different from the church of any other era. Programs are far more complex than in previous years, due to changes in location, surroundings, community, leadership, budget, the price of gas and much more.

4. Some leaders think in their minds: "People will follow me because I am refusing to dismount the dead horse!" Someone has said: "People do things for their own reasons, not yours." Church staff leadership has a difficult time coming to grips with this statement! Rarely do people have hard and fast ties and loyalties to any person, program or event. People will follow their leader as long as they are leading, but loyalties diminish quickly as programs languish with poor attendance, lack of enthusiasm, little creativity and little on the horizon that is promising.

I'm sure you can name programs in your leadership situation that are in danger of becoming a dead horse. Get off as soon as possible before it is too late! Changes can be made, and your leadership will be better because of your willingness to rethink programs, projects and events in the new light of the twenty-first century!

By the way, it has been quoted that by the year 2030, up to half of the churches in the USA will be out of business and their buildings sold. Perhaps this mantra is more important now than ever before.

Mantra Number Six

The person in the organization who communicates clearest the vision is often perceived to be the leader. (Andy Stanley)

Is this ever a true statement! I've been there, and I think perhaps you have been there also. Here are a couple of scenarios:

Scenario One. We are sitting in a staff meeting and the leader (the person in charge, the one charged with the responsibility of this meeting) seems to be in the dark, or not informed, or out-of-the-loop, or on another planet, or all of the above, and our attention is drawn to someone on the team who is giving information that is helpful, useful, needed, and viable to the information on the table. Our minds seem to go automatically to this person as being the "leader," because he/she is in the "know" and seems to have a grasp of the situation.

Scenario Two. We are seated in a church conference, with lots of people present, and the leader is giving away the responsibility to others who seem to be more informed and up-to-date than he is. The person that is stating the facts sways the mood and feeling of the group and providing the kind of leadership expected—and becomes, in our minds, the "leader" of this situation.

Scenario Three. We are in a rehearsal and the leader (conductor, director) is allowing another to direct the rehearsal through comments and opinions that could sway the choir or orchestra to his side of thinking, which may be opposite to the thinking and plans of the director.

Thus, it becomes imperative and absolutely necessary for the leader to be thoroughly prepared, which certainly includes having good information at his fingertips and providing the air of certainty in all discussions. This does not mean, however, that this leader cuts off conversation, suggestions, and the thoughts of others while ruling with an iron hand. This is necessary for good relationships in the meeting, but it does mean that the leader should be the leader and not allow someone else in the meeting, rehearsal or conference to be perceived as the leader.

It is a fine line, but one that must be foremost in the mind of the leader through this process of handling a meeting, conference or rehearsal.

Mantra Number Seven

When you stop asking questions, you stop learning.

Great leaders are great learners.

The Bible has much to say about learning. It tells us everyone should be acquainted with wisdom and continue in the learning process, no matter our age, until we go home to be with Him in the heavenly realm. Proverbs 4:13 says: *"Hold on to instruction, do not let it go; guard it well, for it is your life."*

Proverbs 4:7 says: *"Wisdom is supreme; therefore, get Wisdom. Though it costs all you have, get understanding!"*

2 Timothy 2:15 says: *"Study . . .to show thyself approved unto God . . . a workman that needs not to be ashamed."*

When one continues to learn and grow in wisdom, usually the following takes place:

- There is continuing education on a regular basis.
- There is a continual renewal of basic skills.
- There is a learning of new and/or improved techniques.

These are essential for all ministers, whether they be music, pastors, youth, education, senior adults, singles or children's ministry.

Learning does the following things, and more:

- Broadens the scope of your vision
- Broadens the outlook on life
- Provides the opportunity for continued honing of skills
- Gives a better life experience
- Provides the perfecting of natural abilities that make the person a better and more disciplined minister.

Continual learning stretches the person and his innate skills, makes him more confident and secure in this fast-changing world, and provides opportunity to see beyond self and gets him out of the fortress mentality

One is never too old to be learning something new. There is certain magic and renewing of the personal spirit when one is learning new, exciting and useful tools for ministry.

Thankfully, some churches offer sabbatical leaves or other time off for learning and improvement, and the churches are the richer for it. They receive the direct benefit of the educational process. It is a "win-win" situation for all. If a sabbatical leave is not available, some ministers use their vacation or time away for study and training. Some go to seminars across the country to meet their specific needs. Others go to the local college or university to obtain a special study program on an individual basis in an area of interest with qualified individuals. Some even travel overseas to study. The opportunities are there.

If you feel you have stopped growing and feel the need for a refresher course in your skill areas, get away for a time. Rethink your priorities, calling and ministry. Ask your church for a sabbatical to renew your music and ministry skills and to have the opportunity to be refreshed. Search for new ideas and new techniques that will challenge you. Look for a new challenge. It is not too late.

Mantra Number Eight

Always play to your strengths. Delegate your weaknesses.

You can't do it all.

Sounds so simple, doesn't it? Well, it isn't, and you know this to be true. Many leaders are too concerned about what others will think of their leadership. For instance, if they delegate certain responsibilities to others, their leadership style may be questioned if they don't do everything themselves. That is called micro-management, and it has no place in the leadership in business or the church.

You see, the myth that is so prevalent these days is this: "The good leader has to be good at everything." This is a myth. You do not have to necessarily upgrade your weaknesses into strengths. You can learn how to delegate your weaknesses to others who have strengths in the areas where you are weak. But the moment a leader steps away from the things he does best and tries to do things that he is not qualified to do well, his leadership diminishes, and those who are under such a leader will find their effectiveness suffering also.

Keeping too many balls in the air at one time will create an atmosphere of failure and/or despair for if one drops someone on your staff could have succeeded in keeping one of the failed balls in the air and would have gained self-confidence in the process.

If you, as the leader, feel that no one can handle everything but you, there is a micro-management problem here along with a very large ego. Remember: people who follow us are almost exactly where we have led them, so if there is no one to do all the tasks, it may be our own fault!

Mantra Number Nine

Learn every thing you can from everyone you can whenever you can.

It has been discouraging to me over my years in ministry leadership to discover that so many people receive their college or seminary degree(s) and then, seem to quit learning, experimenting, stretching and growing

Ten Leadership Mantras for Success

in their leadership skills, and then they wonder why they may be floundering in the same old, same old! One should never stop learning. Any person in a leadership position should continue to learn all they can from as many leaders as possible!

You can't sit in an ivory tower office and grow in leadership skills. There is no leadership pill on the market that you can take twice a day and become a positive and strong leader. There is no leadership tonic available as yet!

So how does one learn every thing they can from everyone they can?

It seems so simple! Make a point to attend leadership conferences and workshops as well as read good books on leadership. By the way, I have a very good list of outstanding leadership books that I would be happy to send you, if you will email me your request.

Two of the very best leadership books on the market are:

1. *The Nest Generation Leader, Leadership for the 21st Century,* Andy Stanley, Multnomah Publishers

This is perhaps the most outstanding book for church staff leaders that I have ever read. This is an excellent staff retreat book. Be sure and get a copy! Sadly, this book is out-of-print, but you can still find it on Amazon.com.

2. *The Leadership Labyrinth,* Judson Edwards, Smyth & Helwys

This book ranks right up with the Stanley book. It is an easy read with short chapters, but it is full of good, solid leadership advice. One word of caution: substitute "staff" or "leader" for the word "pastor." The book would have sold better if he had not aimed the text at the pastors, but at staff members and church leaders. Edwards has been in the ministry 36 years and has served only two churches! That says something for his leadership skills. By the way, he is the cousin of Randy and Mark Edwards.

These two books could open a whole new world and a fresh chapter of learning for you who wish to become better, stronger, more effective leaders.

What Think Ye?

Mantra Number Ten

Character is not made in crisis. It is only exhibited.

Character is one of the absolutes for effective leadership. Without this quality, leadership of an individual is severely compromised. More than anything else, followers want to believe their leaders are ethical, fair and honest. Unfortunately, in today's world, it is becoming more and more difficult to uphold one's integrity.

Texas Business editor-in-chief Brux Austin said, "We have been programmed to acquire—at the expense of both our personal integrity and personal fulfillment."

How sad. In today's world, leaders are being strained to the breaking point because of the pressure of leadership with integrity. The good news is that those with proven and sustained character stand out all the more! Those men and women who stand tall, work hard, will not cut illegal corners and profess truth and integrity are leaders whom people will want to follow.

This is especially true in ministry, don't you think? There seems to always be a rash of dismissals among church leadership for a wide variety of reasons, from immoral behavior to financial questions, from "hammer-style" leadership to lack of concern or interest in ministry needs of the flock. Again, how sad. The loser, of course, is the church family, especially those who looked up to their leaders and thought they had integrity and character.

In our fast-paced, ever-changing world, the test of character is displayed almost daily, under pressure, in the "fire" of everyday living and certainly in all aspects of ministry.

Bernice Ledbetter, *Life@Work* (January. 2000), suggests ten ways to build a worthy leadership legacy of character.

1. Focus on relationships! Relationships are the key to success.
2. Create a vision. Every leader must have a vision and be able to pass it on.
3. Champion the truth. Never be one who is suspect in telling the truth.
4. Become personally accountable. People look to you for leadership.

Ten Leadership Mantras for Success

5. Set the bar high for yourself, and others will set their bars higher.
6. Inspire others, and they will look to you for inspiration.
7. Be creative and flexible within the rules; just don't break them!
8. Integrate your work with your beliefs. Stand tall for what you believe and live it in front of your followship.
9. Mentor others. This is your best chance to leave a lasting legacy.
10. Let your work always be an expression of gratitude. Never forget to thank people!

The most valuable tool the servant/minister will have in the twenty-first century will be personal integrity. This means integrity:

- In finances
- In keeping our word
- In all moral issues
- With our families
- With our staffs
- With our friends
- With our Savior.

The new generation of servant/ministers according to Will Beal, will be leaders and not managers. The difference is crucial.

1. Managers administer. Leaders innovate.
2. Managers copy. Leaders originate.
3. Managers maintain. Leaders develop.
4. Managers focus on systems and structures. Leaders focus on people.
5. Managers rely on control. Leaders inspire trust.
6. Managers have short-range view. Leaders develop a long-term perspective.
7. Managers ask how and when. Leaders ask what and why.
8. Managers look at the bottom line. Leaders look at the horizon.
9. Managers accept the status quo. .Leaders challenge it.

What Think Ye?

    10. Managers are company people. Leaders are their own person.

    11. Managers do things right. Leaders do right things.

    12. Managers are helpful. Leaders are essential.

Again, William Easum said in his book, *Dancing with Dinosaurs*: "The best way to fail tomorrow . . . is to try and improve on today's successes."

What think ye?

eight

Worship—Prayer—Church Concepts

The Mystery of Worship

There's no doubt. Those of us in music ministry leadership know how to "do" and prepare corporate worship. We are familiar with the processes, planning, products, details, people and potential that exist in our own local congregations. In short, we've become masters of the management in the mystery of worship, and rightfully so.

There's a degree of legitimate need there. Someone has to take care of the details and we are the ones to do that.

The incident, recorded in 2 Chronicles 5:11–14, provides an example. Read it now, if you will.

As you read the record, it's obvious they didn't just decide, "Hey! Let's meet in 15 minutes and have a worship service!" It says in the Scripture that the people were dressed in fine linen, playing cymbals, harps and lyres, and 120 priests were playing trumpets. It must have been quite a sound. They raised their voices "as with one voice."

That took some doing, or managing, if you will.

Something extraordinary happened that day! God showed up as only He can do. There is something conspicuous in His presence, yet something of mystery as well.

We observe both elements in the story—mystery and management. However, without the element of the mysterious, it might have just been an exercise of management.

What about worship at your place?

What Think Ye?

Does it only display the marks of masters of the management in the worship experience, or does it bear the greater badge of the master of mystery?

What think ye?

The Art of Worship

Regardless of what some may say, there is an art to the worship experience. Worship just doesn't happen. Scripture tells us time and time again that the biblical worship experiences were well-planned and carried out with great fear and trembling as well as excellence.

The art of worship is often a mystery to those who plan it week-after-week, month-after-month. I've asked some of my music ministry friends to share their thoughts on this delicate subject. You may write your comments out as well.

Stephen Lawton, music and worship, Mitchell Road Presbyterian Church, Greenville, S.C.:

> "The art of worship, for us, begins with prayer. The team bows heads before a blank screen-before we presume to compose a worship service. We ask the Holy Spirit to accompany the thoughts and keystrokes that will become congregational worship. We pray for the people, that they can make sense out of it. We ask that even the moments of planning might be true worship. We beg for a fresh view of every element, every Scripture lesson and every word of every song. We ask that God will make art out of our scribbling; we pray that He would help us to exclude all that is pretentious, proud, self-righteous and sanctimonious. By the work of the Spirit, the simple and humble ordinary elements must combine to make something truly extraordinary; with His presence, the whole promises to be infinitely greater than the sum of its parts. Week after week, we are surprised to find this artistry taking place in worship, and so we say thank you once again, not to the liturgist, but to the Artist of our souls."

Michael Adler, minister of music/worship, Shades Mountain Baptist Church, Birmingham, Ala.:

> "I could talk for hours about the hand of God in artistry. I am intrigued by the differences in those who can "see" art and those

who cannot. To see an empty room, a blank canvas, a lump of clay, molten metal—all as potential platforms to display the glory of God—is a profound gift.

"A worship leader has that exact same privilege. To see the human heart as a blank canvas, or even as a piece of art that is not yet completed, is a gift. Worship leaders can see an empty room and know that the simple addition of sounds, light and texture is amazing. What is even more profound is that the heart of man receives the benefit of those artistic additions. A worship leader is also able to color a space and know that one heart will interpret in one way and another may see an entirely different picture

"Worship as art is available to us to use as we wish. It is our duty to be good stewards of that art, to do all we can to create an artistic environment that absolutely compels the viewer to chase after God and to know Him as the Master Designer."

Rich Muchow, former worship leader, Saddleback Community Church, Lake Forrest, Calif. :

"There is definitely an 'art' factor to the corporate worship service. In today's culture with very high expectations, creativity at the speed of thought, high value placed on flexibility combined with limited resources and time, team collaboration is essential.

"Jesus said: *'I am the Vine, you are the branches; he who abides in Me and I in him, he bears much fruit, for apart from Me you can do nothing'* (John 15:5). This verse is foundational for everything we do that honors God, including the art of worship.

"Here is a brief description of how each of our Worship team members contributes:

1. The Holy Spirit's role is direction (service flow, song choice, who is on the platform), connection (purpose of corporate worship is to connect people to God and to each other) and power (changing lives).

2. The Senior Pastor's role is lead worship leader. Our corporate worship service look-and-feel is a direct reflection of his philosophy of ministry. He selects the weekly theme, and his philosophy of ministry is reflected in the sound/feel of the worship service.

3. The role of the creative arts team is to be creative and administrative. Often neglected is the importance of

administration within the creative community. Beyond administration is the exciting challenge for the artist is to create for others/with others. I embrace this scripture: 'Be good friends who love deeply; practice playing second fiddle.' Romans 12:10 (MSG).

Used in Deuteronomy 6:13, the Hebrew word, "Abad" is translated "worship." It means to "work, serve and become a servant or worshipper." This team distributes the work to a manageable level. While some worship leaders try to do all of the work themselves, the most effective way and the biblical way is to let the body of Christ exercise its gifts for the glory of God. Some are singers; some, instrumentalists; some, drama; some, dance; some have the gift of organization, hospitality, promotion and recruiting. The key is building a team from the congregation to the platform!

4. The Tech Team's role is to support all gatherings that benefit from sound, video and lights. Creativity is essential as is training, expertise, administration and service.

5. The role of the congregation should be thought of more as an army than an audience! The staff serves the congregation, not the other way around. The staff's role is five fold: to help the congregation connect with God, know Him, know His people, grow in Him and serve Him. Leading a worship service is obviously much different that performing a concert. The artist is the fire. The worship leader lights the fire.

"The art of worship must incorporate all of the above, not only with each other, but all church teams, and a congregation that is mobilized for ministry."

David Briley, minister of music, First Baptist Church, Decatur, Ala.:

"The 'art of worship' speaks to effective planning, and this is an art form. Mark 12:30 tells us to worship with all of our "heart, soul, mind and strength." This takes careful planning. To experience worship in this way, we must truly use our minds and our strength and put every ounce of heart and soul behind our efforts, not only in the planning, but also in the execution. This is where the art or worship comes in.

"To plan worship (art), one must know the cultural context of their worshiping community, the biblical purposes of worship, and the form and content of worship for your community.

Worship—Prayer—Church Concepts

"Communities and culture are rapidly changing, but the truths of Scripture (content) never change. The art form (planning) needs to include the following:

1. Scriptural truth (content)

2. Involves creative people in the process (brainstorm)

3. Organizes details of implementation (assigning, delegating)

4. Designs orders of worship that are experiential (encountering God with heart, soul, mind, strength)

5. Equips leaders to execute the plan (facilitating a team)

6. Regularly evaluates all of the above (maintaining effectiveness in a rapidly changing culture)."

Kurt Kaiser, composer/arranger, Waco, Texas:

"The Art of Worship: Worship does not just happen. It takes planning. Every Tuesday at 4:00 P.M., our pastor, minister of music, two mentors and I plan the next Sunday's service. It should be seamless stylistically, textually and musically—everything leading to a climactic point. When it happens, it's wonderful. But it does take planning! The purpose of the planning is to lead the worshipper into God's presence."

Bob Hatfield, music/worship, Dawson Memorial Church, Homewood, Ala.:

"To worship is:

"To quicken the conscience by the holiness of God,

To feed the mind by the truth of God,

To purge the imagination by the beauty of God,

To open the heart to the love of God,

To devote the will to the purpose of God."

(William Temple, former archbishop of Canterbury)

"Worship is God's creation. It is at God's initiative that humankind can experience a relationship with the Creator. Worship is a process of revelation and response. As God reveals to persons His holiness, truth, beauty, love and purpose, individuals respond in worship. As a person responds to God's initiative of grace, worship occurs. Authentic worship should encompass the totality of one's being; his or her conscience, mind, imagination, emotions and will.

"God gave to humankind the arts as a beautiful instrument for the expression of worship to the creator. Through the arts, God allows the created to join Him in creative work.

"Three important elements can help in the preparation and leading of beautiful corporate worship expressions:

"Structure: A corporate worship experience is not a "program." It is a "journey." The goal is to move toward a fresh encounter with God. The structure for congregational worship does not have to be rigid or inflexible. It should have room for freedom and spontaneity. It should be painted in broad stokes with room for individual expression.

"Texture and Color: The elements within a worship journey should provide the richness of a beautiful tapestry. Those colors and texture may come in the form of music in a variety of genre, both congregational music and selections presented by specific individuals or groups. The power of oratory, poetry or drama can also be utilized to intellectually and emotionally move the worshiper. Visual arts such as architecture, Christian symbols, stained glass, sculpture and video elements are vivid elements to capture the imagination of the worshiper.

"Flow and Expression: The journey of worship should be as free as possible from barriers and distractions. Within the structure of the service, the worship leader should guide the worshiper from element to element with a sense of freedom and flow that allows for unhindered worship.

"All of these elements require prayer, planning and preparation. Most of all the "artisan" or leader of the worship experience must "ascend to the hill of the Lord with clean hands and a pure heart." We must personally worship the Lord in the beauty of holiness in order to lead others to that experience."

Matt Rexford, worship pastor, Southside Christian Fellowship, Greenville, S.C.:

"An often ignored 'art' lies in the detailed planning of worship. There are so many details that contribute to the overall flow of a worship gathering, and each one should reflect artistic thought and care."

Worship—Prayer—Church Concepts

Paul Hill, worship arts ministry, First Baptist Church, Marietta, Ga.:

> "The very nature of creative beings imago Deo, or in the 'image of (a creative) God' implies that artistic creativity will be the norm for the creatures (us) to worship their creative Creator. To be artistic implies that an idea is motivated first by an impulse to express an idea in a unique and individual way, is then developed in a series of both organized and stream-of-consciousness movements yet allowing changes as the process unfolds, resulting in a unique one-of-a-kind expression that honors the original motivation to express a specific idea. As worship leaders and planners, I believe we are held to a higher standard of expression than merely repeating what happened last week with those gathered to worship this same creative God. The 'fleshing out' of our worship is a living, breathing artistic offering back to a living, breathing creative and artistic God whose artistic imagination defies explanation. As such, we are compelled to exhaust our creative selves in seeking to worship Him artistically."

Hart Morris, former music/worship, Ashbury United Methodist Church, Tulsa, Okla.:

> "Art, in whatever form, is the result of someone's creativity. The 'art' in the 'art of worship' is the same. It is the crafting of an event whose objective it to point attendees toward God.
>
> "Attendance at such an event does not guarantee that worship will occur; but if the preparer approaches worship as a work of art, carefully thought through, planned, prepared and executed, is there not a much greater possibility that it will? Are you not more inspired viewing Michelangelo's David, than my stick figure drawing of a man on a horse?
>
> "An artist crafts her sculpture. He paints carefully, hoping to inspire the viewer at some personal level.
>
> "The 'art' in the 'art of worship' comes down to the planner of the event—the artist—crafting, preparing and executing each detail of the worship event with the sole objective in mind that each element should point those present toward God."

Susan Deal, associate pastor for worship arts, First Baptist Church, Dalton, Ga.:

> "As an artist draws different colors from the pallet to create a work of art, a worship planner has many colors/elements from which to draw to create an atmosphere conducive for worship. Each church is gifted with talented artists—those gifted in proclamation

through the spoken word or music or drama, men and women skilled in playing instruments or creating a painting, children and youth who energetically contribute through singing and dance. We each have the unique privilege and responsibility to offer each of our gifts in the service and worship of God.

"Simple Praise" (Craig Courtney/Pamela Martin)
For the canvas of colors, for the concert of sound,
for the unfolding seasons, the earth spinning round,
for the birth of each sunrise, for the sky set ablaze,
for these simple gifts, we give simple praise.
Simple praise for the Giver and thanks to the One
Who has given us breath and given His Son.
To the giver of blessings for all of our days,
For these simple gifts, we give simple praise.

What think ye?

Three Pitfalls of Worship

There are some pitfalls in worship! I'm sure you have also come to this conclusion. Some times, things go wrong at the right time! We try hard to overcome these obstacles as they appear and try to patch them as best we can with temporary solutions, but some may keep reappearing! It is frustrating, isn't it?

Here are three reoccurring pitfalls that might interest you.

1. Traditional/Contemporary. I have had the privilege of having conversations with two gentlemen who are at the extreme ends of the concept of worship in today's churches.

    The first gentleman is 70 years of age, lives in Virginia, is healthy, strong and does an amazing about of farm work—the difficult kind, with cows, planting and harvesting hay, and much more! He is a believer and loves God. He is very frustrated at this time in his life because he cannot find a church that meets his spiritual needs, so he has quit trying to find a place of worship and only goes rarely.

    My question to him: "Tell me what it is that keeps you from finding the church in this area that fits your needs?

Worship—Prayer—Church Concepts

His long response, edited: "There is one church that we love to attend, but it is 30 miles away, difficult to get to often and we feel we would not have any church community, living 30 miles away. Churches near us are in two categories: the music is either so loud that my ears ache when the service is over or so 'high church' it is blandly boring. I get little from attending. I love to hold a hymnal and sing. I love to hold my bible as the Word is being read. So, I'll just communicate with God on my farm!"

The second gentleman was in his late 20s. He was a professional businessman. In conversation, I asked him why he liked the contemporary service. He said (edited): "I love our contemporary service—the louder and more exciting, the better. I can praise God best in this way. The traditional service is so boring. Who wants to hold a heavy hymnal and sing when one can look on a screen for the words! Maybe when I get much older, my worship experience may change, for now, bring it on!"

My observation: I don't think traditional worship folk will ever truly accept the contemporary worship concept and the contemporary folk will never accept the traditional style of worship. "Blended worship," to my thinking, tends to offend both sides. But, I've been known to be wrong before!

2. Lack of planning is a major worship pitfall. Scripture tells us over and over about the preparations that went into their worship experiences: dance, instruments, singers—lots of all three—and this just didn't happen! It had to be carefully planned. We do the Lord a great disservice when we do not plan worship carefully and ask His blessing in the process. Worship is truly an art form.

3. Same old, same old. As worship leaders, we should never get into the habit of doing the same old, same old in worship week after week. Never just change the hymn numbers and rely on the order of worship that fits your needs. Worship is not about you! Worship is about God and His people. Changing the order of worship often is healthy, keeps the people on their toes and extends their interest in the worship experience. No order of service is OK, if the worship experience doesn't fall into the same style very Sunday! If your worship leaders do the same order every week,

What Think Ye?

> Sunday after Sunday, they need to be called on it and asked why they never do anything creative, innovative or out of the ordinary!

Pitfalls of worship, there are more.

What think ye?

Worship Preferences

I am so sick and tired of hearing the term, "Worship wars!" If I hear it again, I think I will _____ (fill in the blank!). We have about run this one into the ground, don't you think? In addition, another offensive is calling the church choir the "war department" of the church.

The term is about as passé as yesterday's newspaper, the Edsel, bell-bottom trousers, Kodak Moments and _____ (your turn again!).

I think we should begin to use the term, "worship preferences," for that is what worship really is to most people—a preference!

You may prefer Coke over Pepsi, basketball over football, mountains over the beach, blue over green or hymns over choruses, but regardless of your preference, it is still a preference.

If my preference in worship style is traditional, contemporary will probably not ever win me over. If I prefer a contemporary style of worship, traditional will probably never be my preference.

Yet, we continually press our congregations to change their preference of worship style! The church leadership decides, usually with little real input from the congregation, to change the worship style in one or two weeks, going from traditional to contemporary. This decision does not fare well with many of those in the congregation. As a result, many leave to seek their worship preference elsewhere. You may hear terms like, "Good riddance," or "Hope they will be happy now" or even "Now that thorn in my side is finally gone!"

How very sad, both for those that left and for those making the comments. Basically, what happened is this: their worship preference was taken away and communication with and worship of God through their preference was high-jacked.

Think about it this way:

1. Worship preference is a very personal experience. If one is a long-time believer, having grown up with a traditional worship preference, changing their worship preference is not something they will take lightly. It is difficult for them to make the switch and change their preference. At the same time, new believers, having little or no knowledge of hymns, all the "thee" and "thou" words that are not used in language today, and the fast-paced worship of the contemporary experience, this is just right for them. It fits their worship preference, and they probably won't be switching preferences anytime soon!

2. Worship preference does not change because the pastor takes off his coat and tie, is very casual, and makes sure the music is up-tempo and loud. Loud and fast do not worship make! Obviously, many contemporary worship leaders are totally unaware that sometimes, more than half of the congregation is not singing. Why? Two reasons for this are: (1) The leader and praise team are singing so loud that they cannot even hear anyone but themselves. (2) New songs are introduced without any preparation. Most congregations don't do "new" very well, especially with little forewarning.

3. If a church family (note the word, "family" here) decides that the worship preference of the church is to be changed, then preparation, planning and planning, preparation need to be done—slowly and gently, making sure all are on board for this great and mighty change. It may not seem "great and mighty," but believe it! It is! They may not ever say anything about it, but their worship preference has been changed big time and they will not forget it and most will not forgive it.

So, let's drop worship wars and begin to think worship preferences. And let's begin to think of the congregation: their background, what has gone before, and begin to take careful baby steps in desiring to change the worship preferences of the people! We will all be better off!

What think ye?

White to Black

It is very rare indeed that one can go from white to black or black to white, without going though some shades of gray! Common sense is a good teacher, and experience should have taught us those sudden, dramatic and drastic changes in everyday living, daily schedules and even worship experiences will always cause problems. But somehow, common sense has escaped obvious reasoning!

For example, a lady called me some weeks ago, saying that their church was in deep trouble. No surprise here; many are in deep trouble for various reasons. She told me the pastor decided to fire the part-time and faithful music director who had led the church for some fifteen years in a more traditional and slightly blended worship experience, and he had hired a local contemporary musician, who could not read music but played a fair guitar and had led contemporary worship a few times. That, dear readers, is what is known as going from "white to black" in an instant! One Sunday, everything is fine. The next Sunday, the church has a band, no choir, praise team and all the trappings of contemporary worship with absolutely no forethought or preparation.

Needless to tell you, things went sour very quickly. People have left the church in droves; the hired musician has been fired, and they are now looking for a blended worship leader who can lead them to new paths of contemporary glory.

It is rare indeed that a church will go from black to white, meaning going from contemporary worship to traditional worship in a heartbeat or a week's time.

I venture to say that if this church—or any other church that is contemplating worship style changes—must go through various shades of gray to make the transition smooth, less offensive, carried out with professionalism, and of course, asking God's blessings on the changes, which is sometimes, an afterthought.

I also believe that church leadership from many sources has to be involved in these proposed changes from beginning to end, or it is doomed to fail. This is the first shade of gray!

Another shade of gray would be to explain to the congregation on more than one occasion that changes in the worship style and structure will be coming and ask for their input, suggestions and thoughts on this matter. This is vitally important. After all, as someone once told me, "They will be there long after you have gone!" How true, how true!

One last thought on the shades of gray is that the worship personality to begin this process of changing from one color to the next must be one who understands that the success of this change does not depend on his vocal ability, his guitar skills, his use of the microphone or his ability to teach new songs. It depends on his knowledge of where the church currently stands in worship and where the church wishes to go in the worship experience change. He then must be flexible enough to work with the people to make the changes gradual and non-invasive, while at the same time using the "old" along with the "new," and avoiding the pitfalls that come with going too far, too fast and without any preparation.

There is lots more that can be said about drastically going from one color to the next overnight, and this is not the venue to get into all the nuances, but believe me, it is important to trust your people who will be there long after you have left!

What think ye?

The Purist

The dictionary says that a purist is: "a person who insists on absolute adherence to traditional rules or structures, especially in language or style." This is a very accurate description of today's church music scene. Where, you might ask, are you going with this?

There are purists on both sides of the church music scene, don't you think? There are those who are tradition-bound, not free to go outside any lines, take any chances or sing any music that doesn't fall within the tradition boundary lines. There are those who are so "free in the Spirit" that they feel they must try every new idea that comes down the path.

For example, a friend told me recently that while attending a music worship conference, one of the speakers was an organist-choirmaster, and in the Q & A part of his presentation, someone asked: "Have you ever prepared 'My Eternal King,' by Jane Marshall?" His reply: "Absolutely not. I would never present anything to our choir and congregation that did not have organ accompaniment—music written for choir and organ and not adaptations of the piano score." That was quite to-the-point, wouldn't you say?

My initial thought was, "How sad!" How sad that his choir and congregation have never heard or experienced this marvelous Marshall masterpiece. Perhaps, they have yet to experience the powerful effects of "The Majesty and Glory of Your Name," by the choral master, Tom Fettke, because it did not have a specific organ score. Directors can find themselves centering in on one style of music and the purist factor kicks in, saying "a person who insists on absolute adherence to traditional rules or structures, especially in language or style."

On the other side of the fence is the purist who only tackles the contemporary style and will have nothing to do with any music that is outside the contemporary box.

There was a worship leader in another state and city in the land of "far, far away" who believed in his heart that the music he would prepare in his church was only music that had a strong and up-tempo beat. One day, an older member of the church came to him and in a quiet voice, said, "We are coming up on the Easter Season, and would it be too much to ask if the choir might sing 'The Hallelujah Chorus' as part of our Easter Celebration?" Now this worship leader has two music degrees and could have done this without a problem.

His response to her: "No, we don't do that kind of music here. But there is a Presbyterian church two blocks down the street. I'll bet they are doing it, and you can go there to hear it."

Is he not a purist in every sense of the word?

People say contemporary music uses the same words over and over again. Do you realize that "Blessed Be The Name of The Lord" uses this phrase 14 times in four verses or 32 times if all four verses are sung! Recently, we visited a church that has a powerfully effective worship team and a host of instrumentalists who weave the contemporary with the traditional hymns as effectively as any I've ever heard. We did sing one praise chorus from HillSong that repeated the same phrase many times, but I didn't find it offensive in the least. Nor do I mind singing "Blessed Be the Name of the Lord" 32 times, if the worship touches my inner soul!

So, you see, there are purists on both sides of the wide spectrum. And you don't even have to choose sides! Thanks be to God.

What think ye?

Worship—Prayer—Church Concepts

Economy-Driven Worship?

We are currently experiencing unprecedented times of financial strain. Everyone—very family, every business, and every church—is having difficulty meeting budget and/or making ends meet. People are being laid off by the thousands with no end in sight, at least in the near future.

"I already know all this, so what are you trying to say?" you may say.

Good question! *Creator* magazine and *Monday Morning Email* have recently been inundated with emails and letters from church musicians all over the country who are wanting to leave their churches for greener pastures, or who are feeling pressure to leave even if there is no grass in sight, or who are being asked/forced to cut back to one-half or three-fourths time or the position dismissed because offerings have decreased and times in the church are tough.

So is worship so tentative that we use the economy as the reason to cut worship staff and place worship in a secondary position?

Recently, one of my former Samford University students emailed me about an opportunity he had to consider changing churches. He had been contacted by a church and asked if I knew about the church as well as my opinion of the church and my thoughts on what he should do.

In brief, this is what I told him:

- If, after times of sincere and heartfelt prayer with the God who first called you to your present position,

- If you are having a good experience in your present church,

- If, after the number of years you have served this church, the people still love you and respond to your music ministry leadership,

- If you are somewhat free to do your thing without too much interference from pastor and people,

- If you are enjoying your time in this community, stay!

My reasons for telling him this included:

- If you move to this new position and the pastor decides to retire in two to three years (which is the case with this church), or if he decides to move, you will be at the mercy of an incoming pastor who may wish to bring his own music person and you'll be left to fend for yourself. Or the new pastor may want to change the church emphasis to something like "hip-hop religious" and unless you can do this, you'll be looking for a new position, which will be difficult to find in these times!

- If you move to this new position, and financial times continue to get worse, the church may decide to cut staff to a lesser amount of time, which will also include a salary reduction, and you'd be "low person on the totem pole," or the first to cut or go. This could happen in the current situation, but it is unlikely unless times change drastically.

- If you move to this new position, you will be starting over, beginning anew regardless of how successful the previous music program in the church may have been. You will still be the new kid on the block; in your present church, you are considered "the" music minister, "the" music man, "the" music guru, which may or may not be true!

- If you move to this new position, you will be taking your family from roots put down during your time there and new roots are hard to plant regardless of how attractive the situation may be to you. Consider seriously the effect the move will have on your family.

So, to make a long story short, I encouraged him to remain where he was until he began to feel the gentle nudge of the Holy Spirit and had the feeling that God was involved in doing a new thing in his life and ministry, and when this happened, his family would be on board, too.

I also reminded him that the grass may appear greener on the other side in another place, but it still had to be fertilized. This takes hard work, and even then, it may fail. I think he will stay where he is.

What think ye?

Hymns: Yesterday, Today—But Tomorrow?

- Hymns are no longer the main vehicle for today's changing worship scene.

- Hymns mostly speak of another era, certainly not to our contemporary society.

- Hymns are basically boring. All the "thee's," "wilt's," "thou's" and other ancient words leave me cold.

These are statements that I have had spoken in the past years of my life. I do not believe any of these statements—period.

I've heard equal statements about contemporary worship songs, but this is not the theme of this column. That discussion comes next essay.

The theme for now is: "Hymnody . . . will it survive?" What can be done to keep here hymnody alive for the next generation and the one after that? Is anyone writing thoughtful, theological hymns these days, with singable melodies and harmonies that would interest a contemporary culture?

In the midst of all this discussion, a young man from Northern Ireland, shows up by the name of Keith Getty. Chances are you first noticed the name while singing "In Christ Alone." It's the first hymn that the Irish composer/arranger co-wrote with British songwriter/worship leader, Stuart Townsend. Getty grew up singing hymns and metrical psalms in his Presbyterian church. Several experiences, however, tugged him back to his congregational hymn singing roots. His pastor in Belfast couldn't find songs to fit biblical sermons so he asked Getty to write some. Getty noticed that, even in dementia, his grandfather remembered "O Love That Wilt Not Let Me Go," and other hymns he had learned as a child.

Keith and his wife, Kristyn, decided to join their musical talents in creating modern hymns for the church universal—hymns that all ages can sing together in worship. After all, he explained, "What we sing becomes the grammar of what we believe."

He also made this powerful statement: "It's been several hundred years since Christian worship was as shallow as it is today. Christianity is more universal than it's ever been, but people's understanding of their faith and the Bible is disappointing,"

Whether writing hymns with his wife or Townsend, he said two goals guide him:

1. To write theological and Bible truth that speaks in everyday life, as Charles Wesley did.

What Think Ye?

2. To write melodies that large groups of people can sing. That is my filter: Can all ages sing this melody?

He said: "From a lyrical point of view, we use Bible terms in a poetic way—to give the lyrics class and artistic credibility. But we write in language we would speak, that you can imagine saying to someone."

This style doesn't necessarily fit with the Christian music industry. Instead, he is attempting to create hymns for churches to tell the stories of the Bible.

Other contemporary hymn writers are following his lead, writing very strong texts and melodies with contemporary harmonies that speak to all ages in today's culture. My son, David, has a new hymn tune/text in the new and very fine hymnal, *Engraving Grace*. His desire is to provide hymn texts and tunes that can be sung by all generations. His hymn is titled, "*We Find Our Peace*," and here is the first verse:

> "When life comes sideways, twisting, turning,
> Our minds are strained, our spirits churning;
> We turn to God for peace and comfort,
> Our lives best lived in holy concert."

To sum up this brief discussion, think on these things:

- Do you think hymnody is making a comeback in today's churches?

- In planning worship, do you work at providing your congregation a wide variety of the contemporary of today and the hymnology of the ages?

- A person told me recently: "There's no use in buying new hymnals. The texts are on the screen and few people ever pick up the hymnal anymore." Do you agree with this statement?

The modern church is at a critical stage in history. Hard decisions are being made that will affect the future generations as it relates to the depth and theology of hymnody.

What think ye?

Contemporary Music: Here to Stay or Soon Gone?

This essay will discuss the future of contemporary music and see if we can find some middle ground as to whether this style of music is temporary or permanent. This is by no means an intense study or "white paper" on this subject. It is just some ideas to cause us to think—something we need to do more often—rather than being so quick to provide answers.

The debate between hymnody and contemporary worship music is still very much alive. The "great gulf" is still in place, with those who believe in hymnody only on one side and those who stand tall for the contemporary flair on the other. But there is also a huge middle ground, with many people gradually leaving the comfort of being on one side or the other.

The contemporary mystique is becoming more familiar and some drastic changes are taking place in worship experiences. One lady asked me recently, "Why should we buy new hymnals? We always have the words on the screen?" This is happening in many churches; yet, the sales of new and improved hymnals with careful thought to the traditional and the contemporary are gradually increasing.

The contemporary worship songs/hymns/choruses no doubt are getting stronger and more singable, with melodies that will stick in the mind's memory bank, without the constant repetition that occurred in some earlier writings. The writers/composers seem to be centering more on God, Jesus and related subjects that are dear to the hearts and minds of today's church people. Almost gone are most of the "I," "me," "we," and "mine" words. They are being replaced with texts that speak to the whole heart, soul and experience with God, Jesus and the truth of the gospel.

In my days as a minister of music, I would usually prepare to do the following things each week prior to worship and on Sunday morning:

- Prepare the worship service on paper, using information gleaned from the pastor's message and other things/events on the church horizon

- Meet with my pastor for a deep look into the service, to make sure it was on target

What Think Ye?

- Rehearse during the week the choir, bells, orchestra, drama to make sure all were ready on Sunday, arrive early and check with sound, light people, drama, etc.

- Rehearse with organist/pianist and/or instrumentalists

- Rehearse choir and make our entrance.

Today, the minister of music or worship leader or worship pastor seems to do so much more in preparation for worship. I have been privileged of being early in some recent services and sit through all that goes on in a contemporary worship experience, and it is sometimes mind-boggling! I often think of the old car commercial and rephrase it: "This ain't your Father's worship service anymore!"

This includes:

- Check pulpit/stage area to ensure proper placement for all that is going to happen

- Check lighting, sound, video, test microphones, screens and PowerPoint©

- Rehearse worship music with drama, band, orchestra, praise team, solos, keyboards

- Rehearse choir, if there is one

- Give instructions (written, if necessary) to all participants, and go over it thoroughly, ensuring a smooth transition in the worship experience.

Of course, there is much more—and less—depending on the situation, and both styles of worship have many aspects to check off each week to ensure dramatic, heart-felt, God-praising, Jesus-loving, people blessed worship!

I would certainly not predict the future of church music. Everything musical has changed in the past 60 years, changed more than any of us could have ever imagined, and much of it for the good. There was once the "golden age of church music." We are currently in the process of refinement once again, and what will come forth from this refining process will improve our worship experiences, our music and our relationship to God.

I do think contemporary Christian music is here to stay, but it will keep evolving, perhaps, into a bright and shining star that will lead God's people into deeper and more meaningful worship of the true and perfect God.

Some music leaders will stay "way out" in an attempt to be cutting edge; others will transition to a contemporary/blended experience. Some congregations will come along side and grow from each experience.

Some will not and will remain in the process of trying to recapture the "golden age of church music," which will probably never happen again, at least in our lifetime.

You have heard both sides of the music styles that are causing controversy in our churches these days. No, it has not died down. There are still strong feelings both ways.

What think ye?

Thirteen Critical Issues for the Twenty-First Century Leader

1. Assimilation of potential

2. Change management and continuous learning

3. Technology advancing more rapidly than imagined

4. True spirituality and commitment to God alone

5. Visionary leadership with future focus

6. Interpersonal relationships and skills

7. Less Program Tuft and more integrated programs

8. Designs a comprehensive mission/purpose statement

9. Variety of worship styles

10. Leadership training and mobilization of key leadership

What Think Ye?

11. Reaching younger generations and adults

12. Breaking the 75-100 attendance barrier in church attendance

13. Effective communication with constituency

What think ye?

Creative Ways to Pray

In the *Presbyterian Book of Order*, these words are found:

> "When artistic creations awaken us to God's presence, they are appropriate for worship. When they call attention to themselves, or are present for their beauty as an end in itself, they are idolatrous. Artistic expressions should evoke, edify, enhance, and expand the worshiper's consciousness of the reality and grace of God."

Artistic creations do indeed have the power, beauty and majesty to evoke, edify, enhance and expand the mind and consciousness of any worshiper to both the reality and grace of God. God Himself gave His people the power of the artistic spirit to be used to honor Him, glorify Him and make His greatness known to all.

Dorothy Day asked quite a question: "Whoever said that words were the only way to pray?"

Like many of you, I have prayed through the spoken word many times. But I have also prayed perhaps more meaningful prayers through the creation of music. There have been times, though not often enough, I have found myself weeping after writing a particular choral section or a setting of a handbell composition. It isn't something one shares often with others publicly, but I know many of you have shared prayers through the means of artistic creations.

I remember vividly in the mid 1980s, The Baptist Festival Singers were performing in Notre Dame Cathedral in Paris. As they began to sing the "Doxology," I noticed the choir members were not watching me, and I became aware of tears flowing from many eyes as the singers looked over my head and experienced the beauty of the Rose Window, placed there in the twelfth century and has never had to be repaired or shored up for safety. It is a truly work of artistic beauty, and that artistic expression

Worship—Prayer—Church Concepts

melted the hearts and caused tears of prayerful joy in the faces of high school and college young people on that special day. That was a prayerful moment for me.

On a similar tour with the same group, I found myself weeping tears of joy when the pastor of the International Baptist Church, Salzburg, Austria, came down the aisle at the end of our concert and presented to me a plaster of Paris head of the young Beethoven. The pastor had told me earlier that he had found this in a flea market near the church and had paid about $3 for it. I begged him to give it to me as I dressed for the concert, and he flatly and repeatedly refused. When he presented it to me in front of the singers, I felt it was a "thanks offering poured out to honor the Lord" and given to me as a true artistic love gift. I still have it displayed in our home.

I openly shed tears and pray every time I hear these convicting words by Ken Medema, from his work, "Moses": "What do you hold in your hand today? To what or to whom are you bound? Are you willing to give it up right now? Give it up. Let it go. Throw it down."

M.C. Richards said these words: "All of the arts we practice are apprenticeships. The big art is our life. We must, as artists, perform the acts of life in alert relation to the materials present at any given instant. Art is a moral eye that opens and closes, helping us to see truly."

A great part of the aura of the arts is the challenge to learn to "be still and know that I am God." We are far too busy today to be still and know anything!

But when one is creating art with the potter's wheel, one can become quiet in prayerful thought of family and friends.

When one is painting a canvas, splashing the colors and creating a work of art in the process of being still can cause praying in new and creative ways.

Whether one is using a paintbrush, pieces of cut glass, a set of colored pencils, sticks of chalk, manuscript paper, a piano keyboard, an instrument of brass, percussion or wind, in process of writing a book, making candles, creating scrapbooks, dancing for and before God, or literally hundreds of other ways of artistic expression, all these can be times of prayerful expressions of thanksgiving, grace and beauty.

Whoever said that words were the only way to pray?

What think ye?

What Think Ye?

Where Were These Words Spoken?

1. "Greetings! How are you today?"

2. "Hello! I'm so very pleased you are with us today. How can I assist you?"

3. "I'm so glad you came in today. If there is anything I can do, let me know."

4. "Can I help you find your way around? Are you looking for something specific?"

Having served for eight years as director of church music, Florida Baptist Convention, Jacksonville, Fla., and having had multiple opportunities to visit many churches during past years, I wish I could tell you that the four statements above came from the churches I visited and were the way I was greeted and that these comments are typical of all churches.

But I must tell you this is not true. Where do you think these statements were made? Here are the answers:

1. Sam's Club

2. Wal-Mart Super Store

3. Target Super Store

4. Bi-Lo Grocery Store

I have been in church after church in the past few years where not one person has spoken to me, acknowledged my presence or gave me any direction.

Once in a while, I'd get a nod and "Hello," but the person would pass on by. Occasionally, I'd get a "Welcome. Are you a visitor?" When I replied, "Yes," their reply was "Glad to have you today," and the person would continue on their way. It was rare indeed that I was warmly greeted, made to feel welcome or asked if I needed directions to any place in particular.

Now don't misunderstand me! I wasn't looking to be recognized, pampered or royally welcomed. These people didn't know me from Adam's housecat. To them, I was just a person whom they did not know.

Remember: these days, it is rare indeed if someone comes to a church by himself/herself, without invitation and being accompanied by a church member, but it does happen.

Therefore, the church family should be keenly aware of making people feel at home, welcomed and make sure they know where to go, even if it's to the nearest restroom!

I think our people can and should do a better job of welcoming people to their churches, don't you?

What think ye?

Princess Diana and Mother Teresa

A few years ago in the *Florida Times Union*, the daily newspaper for Jacksonville, Fla., the following letter was sent to the editor from Peter Kenny, an auditor, who lives in Jacksonville:

> "Recently, two rather prominent women died. The similarities and contrasts are striking.
>
> "One was a celebrity. One was celebrated.
>
> "One was a biological mother who preferred the title, 'Her Royal Highness.' One seems quite happy to be called 'Mother.'
>
> "One never wore the same dress twice. One always wore the same style clothing.
>
> "One walked with kings. One walked with the King of kings.
>
> "One left an estate valued at some 65 million dollars. One left two pairs of sandals, a water bucket, a rosary, and a well-worn Bible.
>
> "One was a candle in the wind. One was a beacon."

What think ye?

This Isn't Your Father's Oldsmobile, or The Church as We Know It May Be in Trouble

Do you remember that commercial of several years ago where General Motors was trying to convince the younger generation that the newer

What Think Ye?

Oldsmobiles were updated, slick and "not your father's Oldsmobile." They don't make this car any longer. How about the new line of Cadillacs? The ads are appealing to younger generations and the old stodgy line is all but gone.

"So, how does this relate to today's church," you ask.

In August 2008, I attended Promise Keepers 2008 in the New Birth Missionary Baptist Church near Atlanta. This church has 25,000 members and has two Sunday services, each averaging in the neighborhood of 10,000. It is a fine facility, led by a very dynamic pastor, having served there for 22 years.

In the two days, 9,000 men were present. An outstanding worship team led us in singing both dynamic and memorable praise choruses as well as standard hymns done in praise & worship style. There were 9,000 men singing these songs of Zion heartily and fervently. It was a sound to behold, and many times I just stood and listened, letting my heart be refreshed to my very soul.

We heard dynamic and soul-moving messages by outstanding men of God. What was most interesting to me was that in each message, each speaker mentioned the church and where it stands in America today.

So, where do you think the church stands today?

- Is the church of today following biblical principles?
- Is the church of today moving forward, growing, winning non-believers to Christ as they teach the Bible, teach doctrine and grow leadership?
- Is the church of today interested in folks who don't look, act, smell or think like the members do?
- Is the church of today doing the same old same old routine, sticking with programs that are out-of-date and not drawing lost people or even dedicated people?

Here are some comments for consideration, gleaned from the speakers:

We were told that 70 percent of men in today's churches in the America are involved in some way with pornography. Sadly, many of these are church leaders as well as pastors and staff members. How can pastors preach the love of Jesus and how can men lead in the church today if they spend much of their spare time on the Internet surfing pornography sites? How can staff members teach godly principles while being a slave to pornography? Godly leadership is difficult to find or is missing in many churches!

A survey was taken at Promise Keepers, on the spot with cell phones, and results were put on the screen in real time. The number one problem of the men present was pornography. Second was drugs. Third was neglect of their families.

Dwight L. Moody said: "If I walk with the world, I can't walk with God." Truer words were never spoken.

Homes without fathers are causing havoc in today's culture and society, and the church is doing little or nothing about it. The largest people group in the world today that needs our help, love, care and compassion is the single mother who is trying to raise their children without a father figure. When is the church going to wake up to this reality and begin a ministry to them? Believe me, this people group is near every church in the country.

Sadly, there are few pastors in churches who are committed to excellence, and as we recall from Scripture, God demands our best, in worship as well as in the giving of tithes and offerings or service. Many pastors as well as worship leaders seem more content to please the congregation and make sure the boat doesn't rock rather than to preach, teach, sing the words of God and drive them straight to the hearts of God's people. The main theme of many churches is evangelism when most of those in the pews are already believers. There is little preached on how to live a godly life from Monday to Sunday, witness in the marketplace of life, be godly parents, hear God's voice and other profound subjects that are so desperately needed in today's culture.

We will pay the price for churches that are not true to the teachings of Jesus, leadership that is godly on the outside and impure on the inside and ignoring obvious problems around the church and community. If not now, soon.

What think ye?

What Think Ye?

Disney versus Church

When our grand-twins were eight years old, we took them and their parents on a three-day Disney cruise on the good ship, *Wonder*. It was a great experience to see the Disney Magic through the eyes of our grandchildren. We had a wonderful time.

Let me share some observations:

- We were welcomed on board the ship by the captain, who announced our names over a loud speaker and all the staff applauded and welcomed us as we crossed the entrance, as if we were expected!

- Every time we passed or talked with an employee, no matter what level the job, each one would speak and ask how they could be of any assistance.

- Any time we used the phone, we were called by our name and made to feel so very welcomed. (I know our names were on the screen! But it sure felt good.)

- Meals were such a delight. Of course, the food was excellent, and the service and the waiters made each meal an experience. After a few moments, our servers knew us by name, took care of our every need and recognized us the next meal.

We've also been to Disney World several times, and this was our second Disney cruise, the first one with my daughter and her family. Every time we have been involved with Disney World, we have also encountered deeply committed Christian employees who were not afraid to share their faith in conversation. We have been very impressed with this each time we have experienced their freedom to share the Gospel.

As I pondered the cruise and the park, and also being a churchperson, I could not help but relate the experience to the church in general. These were some of my ponderings:

- How delightful it would be if the church visitor's center would welcome people, announce their arrival to church members standing by and then have someone personally take care of them, making sure that visitors were escorted to a class and introduced or escorted to the nursery or sanctuary.

Worship—Prayer—Church Concepts

- What would happen if church members as well as staff would actually would stop and speak to people they did not know, asking if they could be of any help?

- What if, when people called the church, they were made to feel the church receptionist really cared about their needs and was knowledgeable about who was where, what was happening and could answer the questions asked, and if not, transferred the caller to someone who could answer the questions? And would it not be nice to sometimes talk to a person instead of a recording?

- What if, at church fellowship meals, we didn't sit together in our own little clique, but would sit with people we did not know or did not know well? This is a very uncomfortable thing to do for many people, me included. I'm basically a shy person; I find it difficult to do this, but I'm going to give it a try.

- What if we, who are church-related believers, would consistently be so open and free to share our faith with those with whom we come in contact—at the post office, the check-out line at the stores, the cleaners and myriads of other places? It just might make a difference.

As most of us know, a Disney experience is all about make-believe. The Christian life is not! Most of the time, Disney provides a niche for their guests. Remember, to really feel at home in a church of almost any size, there needs to be a niche where people can fit in. That niche might be choir, orchestra, a Sunday School class, a fellowship or a small group within the church. We can't know everyone and sometimes, it is difficult to know new members from visitors, especially if your church has more than one service.

But remember, people like to be called by their names, so it behooves us, especially those who are on a church staff, to learn names and be able to recall those names when necessary.

It sure was a good reminder of how things could be in the church if we made people feel more at home!

What think ye?

What Think Ye?

A New Species of Worship Leader Has Emerged

Here are some thoughts on emerging worship leadership, by Rev. John Simpson, General Superintendent, Baptist Union of Victoria, Australia, with "tongue in cheek:"

- *Enthusiasticus* is joyful and excited to a degree often unattainable by most on a Sunday morning or evening, for that matter! *Cheerleadicus* might be a better name.

- *Spurgeonus* seems to be a frustrated preacher who offers lengthy homilies between songs. Bring your knitting; one could actually get the front of a jumper done before the sermon. This is especially true of soloists who insist on giving their personal insights on each song whether relevant or not.

- *Aerobus* is obviously a fitness video junkie who wants all worshippers to clap, stamp, sway, raise hands, dance and be in on the action. Look for the signs in the foyer warning those with heart conditions, pregnant women and children under five to be careful.

- *Watchlus* has no concept of time. He plans to sing through the entire set of overhead transparencies in one sitting (or standing) regardless of time or energy of the people.

- *Crippilus* insists that everybody should stand for a minimum half hour while two or three songs are sung in "7/11" style, which means 7 verses and 11 key changes. Unfit worshippers crumple after about 15 minutes or two songs, whichever comes first.

- *Confusus* loves new songs and teaches several every Sunday. This person prefers complicated melodies and rhythms but seems to completely ignore vacant stares or total cacophony. The latter passes for "singing in the Spirit."

- *Spiritus* leaves it to the Holy Spirit to guide in the selection of songs as the service begins to unfold. This might account for missing overheads, mental and musical breakdowns at the keyboard and general disarray. Actually, the Holy Spirit probably has had no part in these proceedings at all.

- *Triumphalus* prefers songs of wealth, health, victory and steers clear of songs about the cross, suffering and servanthood, as no one needs to be down today.

- *Mysticus* leads the music with eyes closed, a "Mona Lisa" expression on the face, and body in semi-kneeling position. Possible extreme lower back pain may be the problem.

What think ye?

Hymnody

I must confess that I am becoming very burdened about what I am seeing, feeling and experiencing in worship these days in many churches. Many things are different, even unusual and, for a lot of people, very uncomfortable. Let's look at one such item.

Here are some thoughts on hymns.

Hymnody defines your denomination. Hymnody determines and reinforces your theology, faith and history. We are who we are because of our theology. The theology of your church is found in our strong and beloved hymns. Hymns are memorized and cherished by many.

In his booklet, *Songs for all Seasons,* Chuck Swindoll wrote: "It's amazing how those grand theological truths woven through each stanza of a hymn took up permanent residence in my heart and mind. Even today, I keep a dog-eared hymnal on my desk and in my times with the Lord, I often turn to one of those old standbys and allow the familiar strains to fill my heart again."

Churches that are choosing to not include the great hymns of the faith in the worship experience are not allowing their people to learn and sing the basic truths of their church heritage, whatever denomination you are.

There are also churches who sing no hymns whatsoever. How sad for their people. There is something to be said for tradition.

Many churches no longer use a hymnal, and there are texts in some hymnals that are contrary to the beliefs of your denomination. If a church uses a hymnal that is not from your denomination, the worship leadership needs to be absolutely sure the texts of these hymns gel with the denominational theology.

What Think Ye?

There is a major decline of harmony singing in our churches these days. Most people can't sing harmony to words on the screen. Why? They just aren't "musician" enough to do so. Part of the joy and fun in congregational singing is to sing harmony, and screens do not allow this for only the text is there and no parts are available. Both are available, as you probably know!

Middle and older adults, if they were honest, would say that they are very uncomfortable being forced to sing everything from a screen. Believe it or not, they miss holding the hymnal and singing harmony from the hymnal. Some churches use the screen for choruses and the hymnal for hymn singing; that is a good idea! Why not try a combination of both?

A cappella singing is almost a thing of the past in America church settings. Why? Several reasons come to mind:

1. What we're singing in our services is melody and very little harmony.

2. We are led to believe that the praise band/team will "help" us sing better. Not true.

3. Music that is fast and loud doesn't sound good a cappella.

Someone told me recently that in his church, "If we can't line-dance to it, we don't sing it!" How sad!

People do not like to stand and sing for 15 minutes or more at a stretch—period! If you don't believe that statement, ask your people! They will tell you quickly that it's too long to stand for one given period. After a brief time, energy begins to wane and the singing becomes less and less enthusiastic. Take time to listen to your people. This is especially true if the congregation is largely composed of older adults. People can sing well if seated.

Worship services that carefully and thoughtfully blend choruses and hymns are reaching most of God's people. Believe it!

In a Lord's Supper recently, the leader allowed us to sing spontaneously for about 20 minutes as we prepared our hearts and minds to take the Lord's Supper together. It was amazing to me that we started with a chorus and ended with a chorus, but the remainder of the time, hymns were sung spontaneously, tearfully and with great emotion and confidence. It was a very moving experience.

I urge my brothers and sisters not to discard completely the hymns of their faith. Sing them regularly, even with the praise team/praise band, even with updated charts, but sing them and allow your people to worship through the beauty and theology of the great hymn of the past and the new hymns of present.

What think ye?

Creativity

Here are some penetrating questions that might cause you to do some serious thinking and/or soul-searching:

- Why is there so little creativity in the marketplace and church today?
- Why is there a crisis of creative leadership in today's marketplace and in the church?
- How can people of faith in a creative world—designed by a Creator God—packed with creative people—do so little that is really creative?
- Why do leaders seem to do the same thing, the same program concept and the same music year after year and think their people don't realize that basic creativity is lacking?

Leonard Sweet has said: "Creativity is not coming up with something new from scratch. Creativity is scratching something new out of the old!"

There's a sign on a very long bridge in Florida that reads: "It is against the law to run out of gas on this bridge."

Perhaps, it should be against the law to run out of creativity, innovation and spiritual energy in the marketplace and church before our time runs out!

Creativity is a function of survival!

What think ye?

www.ingramcontent.com/pod-product-compliance
Lightning Source LLC
Chambersburg PA
CBHW072152160426
43197CB00012B/2349